Brief Lives

W. F. Deedes is the only person ever to have been both a Cabinet Minister and a national newspaper editor. He was a minister in Harold Macmillan's administration and later became editor of the *Daily Telegraph*. He frequently appears on television and radio and has recently run high-profile anti-landmine campaigns. He is ninety-two years old and is the author of *Dear Bill*, his Fleet Street memoirs, and *At War With Waugh*.

Also by W. F. Deedes

DEAR BILL

AT WAR WITH WAUGH:
The Real Story of *Scoop*

W. F. DEEDES

Brief Lives

PAN BOOKS

First published 2004 by Macmillan

This edition published 2005 by Pan Books
an imprint of Pan Macmillan Ltd
Pan Macmillan, 20 New Wharf Road, London N1 9RR
Basingstoke and Oxford
Associated companies throughout the world
www.panmacmillan.com

ISBN 0 330 42639 7

1 3 5 7 9 8 6 4 2

A CIP catalogue record for this book is available from
the British Library.

Typeset by Intype London Ltd
Printed and bound in Great Britain by
Mackays of Chatham plc, Chatham, Kent

Contents

Introduction

THIS BOOK IS ABOUT some of the people I have encountered during a long life in journalism and politics, and I have put it together in the belief that they have something to tell us. But in order to understand them it is important to place them in the context of their times rather than judge them by contemporary standards, so it helps to remember those times.

Even the bizarre Imelda Marcos becomes easier to fathom if you remember the cold war and those years when the United States of America and the Soviet Union eyed each other darkly across the Pacific Ocean. The air and naval bases which the Americans rented from the Philippines seemed of such importance to them as to justify indulging the whims of the corrupt President Ferdinand Marcos and his extravagant wife.

We may wonder how on earth someone like Oswald Mosley came to loom so large in our national life. To understand it, you have to recall the state we were in during the years of the Great Depression 1929–32 and the mood that this engendered. Foolish travellers assured us that the Soviet Union was doing well under Communism; Mussolini and his Fascists were putting Italy back on her feet; Germany was about to hail Hitler. Here our staple industries were crumbling, our exports declining, our unemployment close to the three million mark from a smaller workforce than today's. Not just capitalism but parliamentary government itself seemed to be faltering. Who could deliver us? That was part of Mosley's appeal.

But I have also chosen four leading political figures of the last century who, in my opinion, have received less than their due. All four were great public servants yet are vaguely remembered by many to have been flawed. Ramsay MacDonald, Labour's first Prime Minister, has gone down in history in the minds of many Labour loyalists as a man who betrayed his party. Stanley Baldwin, a great Conservative Prime Minister, is unfairly remembered as a man who, by putting electoral considerations first, failed to rearm his country soon enough against Hitler. The label of failure has also been pinned onto Anthony Eden and Rab Butler, whom I first knew in their early days of promise and later served with in different administrations: Eden because of the Suez fiasco, Butler because he twice missed reaching the top of the greasy pole. By any reckoning all four were serious players in the political life of this country; to see them as failures and losers is absurd.

Helen Suzman of South Africa and the late Lilo Milchsack are here because I see them as patriots. By setting up what became known as the Königswinter conferences on the Rhine soon after the Second World War, Milchsack did much to encourage in this country a better understanding of Germany's post-war, post-Hitler difficulties. Suzman, for some years a solitary member of the Liberal Opposition to South Africa's Nationalists, did her bit in bringing apartheid to an end and so helped to make her country acceptable to the modern world.

I came to know Field Marshal Montgomery after the war, when the only platoon commander in my rifle company to survive the battle for Europe, Andrew Burnaby Atkins (MC and bar), became his aide-de-camp. Where Monty stands among the great generals of history, it is not for me to say, but he gave us a welcome victory at Alamein at a crucial point in the war. He was lively in conversation. So was Mary Whitehouse, who was not half as stuffy as her enemies made out. She dealt with those who insulted her with humour and immense bravery.

Malcolm Muggeridge became a friend after we both returned from the war to work for the *Daily Telegraph.* For someone resettling his life after five years of war, he was a good counsellor, though incurably pessimistic; Malcolm believed rather too earnestly in the Fall of Man. I thought of him fondly in 2003 when his daughter Sally arranged a lunch at the Garrick to mark the centenary of his birth. Speaking of Malcolm, Cardinal Cormac Murphy-O'Connor mentioned his attempted suicide on the coast of Mozambique during a fit of wartime depression. His spiritual faith, the Archbishop told us, had saved him. Malcolm had set out to drown himself, but after walking a long way out the water was only up to his knees and he thought better of it and returned. 'So it was part spiritual, part tidal . . .' I replied to the Archbishop, and hoped Malcolm would enjoy the joke.

Edmund Hillary, in 1953 the first man to climb Everest, and Roger Bannister, who ran the mile in under four minutes a year later, rank by contrast to Muggeridge as optimists of my time. Both refused to accept that there was any real obstacle to climbing higher or running faster than man had ever climbed a mountain or run a mile before. Exceptionally strong legs and lungs helped them along, but it was their cast of mind that got them there. They embody man's unending quest for the almost unattainable.

Is there anything fresh to say about Diana, Princess of Wales? I think there is if you remember the abdication of King Edward VIII, and compare how quietly the news media covered that event and how roughly they reported Diana half a century later. Royalty without deference has become an exacting occupation.

I am strongly in favour of *Private Eye* – it did, after all, make me famous with Denis Thatcher's spoof letters to Bill. But one is enough. The magazine's success has attracted imitators. An overdose of cynical comment has brought politics into contempt. As Roger Bannister recalls from his days at Oxford in 1946, 'politics was regarded as possibly the finest career . . . demanding intelligence, ability and a willingness to take risks.' No longer. And in this mood of disenchantment we have come to doubt whether those who served us in the past have much to impart. I differ. Whether they got it right or wrong, they serve as guideposts. That is what makes them worth writing about.

Stanley Baldwin

WINSTON CHURCHILL DENOUNCED STANLEY Baldwin in *The Gathering Storm*, first volume of his account of the Second World War, by reminding us of what Baldwin had told the House of Commons in November 1936. Accused by Churchill of neglecting this country's defences, Baldwin had replied with what he admitted was 'appalling frankness' that he could think of nothing more likely to lose him the 1935 general election than seeking a mandate to rearm. 'This was indeed appalling frankness,' thundered Churchill in his account of the war. 'It carried naked truth about his motives into indecency. That a Prime Minister should avow that he had not done his duty in regard to national safety because he was afraid of losing an election was an incident without parallel in our Parliamentary history.'

That sounds damning unless you remember, as I do, what political feeling was like in Great Britain in the years 1931–5. There was not a cat in hell's chance of persuading this country to enter an arms race with Germany. Churchill, as an independent Member of Parliament receiving reliable information about German rearmament, had every right to sound the alarm, but had he been in Baldwin's shoes at No. 10 and sought a mandate to match Germany's illicit air, naval and military build-up, he would certainly have lost the 1935 election. What then? Would a Labour government, vehemently opposed to 'great armaments', have met the challenge? 'Labour will support no great armaments,' the party's leading figures were declaring.

As Baldwin observed in his controversial speech, 'there was probably a stronger pacifist feeling running through this country than at any time since the war'. In June 1935 we had the Peace Ballot, organized by Lord David Cecil, in which 11.5 million votes were cast in favour of adherence to the League of Nations' policy of collective security and ten million for a reduction in armaments. At its conference in 1932 the Labour party had declared its unqualified hostility to the arming of any country in any circumstances and there had been an extraordinary by-election at East Fulham in 1933, where I spent a day or two as a reporter for the *Morning Post.* The Labour candidate John Wilmot made disarmament the main issue of the campaign; his opponent Alderman Waldron, who pleaded for the maintenance of British defence, was denounced as a warmonger. George Lansbury, the Labour party leader, sent a message to the constituency: 'I would close every recruiting station, disband the Army and disarm the Air Force. I would abolish the whole dreadful equipment of war and say to the world: "Do your worst."' When polling day came a Conservative majority of 14,000 was been turned into a Labour one of almost 5,000. After a war in which nine million soldiers, sailors and airmen had been killed and five million civilians had perished, another war with Germany was widely regarded as unthinkable. Furthermore, though Germany was rearming, Hitler in 1935 did not appear to pose the immediate threat to world peace that he posed just before Munich in 1938.

To all of which the reasonable man might say that Baldwin should still have acted in the best interests of his country, defied public feeling and improved our defences. But this is what Baldwin had tried to do a decade earlier – and failed. In 1923, not long after taking office as Prime Minister, he had decided it was imperative for this country to defend itself against foreign imports by raising tariffs. High taxation had increased the cost of production, the foreigner was underselling us in our own home market and unemployment was rising. Bonar Law, Baldwin's predecessor, had a year earlier promised electors there would be no fiscal changes, so the only course open to Baldwin to secure what he considered the best interests of this country was to call an election on the issue of protection. He did so and lost office, though not for long. By 1924 an inexperienced Labour government had fallen over its own feet and the Conservatives had returned to office. But the protection against cheap imports that Baldwin wanted was not introduced until 1932 when unemployment exceeded two million.

So Churchill's condemnation of Baldwin, which has tarnished his reputation ever since, needs to be weighed. What also should be weighed is the question posed by G. M. Young, who was invited by Baldwin to write his biography. 'We are proud, and rightly proud,' Young wrote in his preface, 'of our unity in 1939 and in the terrible years that followed. Are we sure that without Baldwin that unity could have been achieved, and maintained?' That is my theme.

Baldwin came from what might be called manufacturing gentry; he was an ironmaster's son brought up within sight of the Worcestershire hills. He was not therefore entirely the countryman he sometimes affected to be, but he drew strength from the English countryside. Educated at Hawtrey's preparatory school, Harrow and Cambridge, where he scored a third, he showed little early promise but, after a spell with the family business, entered politics and upon the death of his father Alfred Baldwin inherited the safe seat of Bewdley. Entering the Commons at the age of forty-one in 1908 and speaking only five times in his first six years, he seemed set for a humdrum political career, so much so that he considered quitting Parliament altogether and returning to the family business, which was flourishing on wartime contracts.

Bonar Law, Chancellor of the Exchequer, then made Baldwin his parliamentary private secretary and in June 1917 appointed him financial secretary to the Treasury, a post often seen as a stepping stone into the Cabinet. Two years later Baldwin wrote an anonymous letter to *The Times*, dwelling on the dangerous financial state of the nation after the First World War and the need to do something about it. We were heavily in debt. Estimating the value of his private fortune at about £580,000, he undertook to donate 20 per cent of this massive sum towards the reduction of the war loan. It turned out to be an example which few followed, but it throws light on his enigmatic character. He apparently wished to remain anonymous yet signed the letter with the initials FST – for financial secretary to the Treasury, the post he still held in government.

The turning point in his career came in April 1921 when at the age of fifty-four he was promoted to President of the Board of Trade in the coalition government under Lloyd George. There were no great expectations of him among senior ministers but the House of Commons took a liking to his patience and good humour and felt they could trust him. That element of trust counted, for in the autumn of 1922 strained relations within Lloyd George's coalition came to breaking point. The Liberal party was in tatters while the Conservatives were increasingly restless under Lloyd George, and divided about his value to them. Baldwin had been tramping round Aix-les-Bains, his favourite holiday resort, brooding over his party's future. He decided that the Tories must detach themselves from Lloyd George and his wily ways, and return to responsible parliamentary government. Behind this decision lay profound anxiety about the future of his party rather than promotion of himself.

Baldwin prepared his ground by consulting Conservative colleagues, though up to the last moment he did not know how some of them would respond. As G. M. Young has observed, what Baldwin's speech to Conservative backbenchers at the Carlton Club in 1922 did disclose, though not everyone realized it at the time, 'was that this countrified business man, who seemed to have reached the Cabinet by accident, was the master, and the unequalled master, of a new eloquence: direct, conversational, monosyllabic: rising and falling without strain or effort, between the homeliest humour and the moving appeal.' Baldwin's simple earnestness carried the day. The coalition broke up. Lloyd George resigned. The Conservatives won the 1922 election and Bonar Law, though a sick man, became Prime Minister and appointed Baldwin as his Chancellor of the Exchequer. However, any sense of triumph was soon dimmed by the task of negotiating settlement of the American debt. But Baldwin took a stride forward with his speech on the Address which closed with these words:

> The English language is the richest in the world in monosyllables. Four words of one syllable each . . . contain salvation for this country and the whole world, and they are Faith, Hope, Love and Work. No Government in this country today which has not faith in the people, hope in the future, love for its fellow-men, and will not work and work, and work, will ever bring this country through into better days and better times, or will ever bring Europe through or the world through.

The House of Commons had not heard language like that for a long time. Baldwin followed this up with a Budget speech which was sound, entertaining and, some thought, brilliant. He used his mastery of plain English as a key to the hearts of Members of Parliament – and many outside Parliament. Baldwin spent a long time thinking over what he proposed to say, though speeches were usually delivered from rough notes, never a script. I can remember watching him from the press gallery as he sat on the government front bench apparently idly browsing through the Order Paper while the House was engaged in business outside his area. He did this to escape from his office, the telephone, the private secretaries, colleagues and visitors and thus earned a reputation for indolence. But these spells in the Commons gave him a sensitive ear for other Members' feelings, which is why some of his speeches caught their imagination. They also gave him the chance to think things over quietly. These days the Prime Minister is expected to be perpetually in motion and action; he has no time to ruminate. 'My mind moves slowly,' Baldwin sometimes remarked. What he then had to say was all the better for it.

He understood his countrymen, not merely those he associated with in business and politics, but the working man and woman; and, as many of his speeches showed, he had insight into their thoughts and aspirations. I once heard him speak at Ashridge, which was then a Conservative college. The *Morning Post* had sent me there disguised as a student to report on whether the teaching was true blue. Baldwin's contribution was a bit of a ramble, but his earnest tone of voice drew you into what he was saying. I do not think I ever heard him utter a cliché.

So when ill health compelled Bonar Law to retire Baldwin was a serious contender for the premiership. His main rival was Lord Curzon, who, though Baldwin's senior, was a controversial choice as it would mean a Prime Minister sitting in the House of Lords. Baldwin also had his drawbacks: he was not well versed in foreign affairs nor greatly interested in them and he was not well known, partly because he disliked publicity. Baldwin himself had doubts. To a journalist who congratulated him on the steps of No. 10, the new Prime Minister replied, 'I need your prayers rather.' He took to a cherrywood pipe, wore the incongruous mix of a wing collar with a tweed jacket and waistcoat and took over a nation in a delicate state of health.

The war had played havoc with our overseas trade. Britain had not become, as Lloyd George had promised, a 'land fit for heroes'; on the contrary, many of the heroes were out of work. Baldwin took the plunge, dissolved Parliament and sought a mandate for protection. His miscalculation meant that the Tories lost but neither the Liberal nor Labour parties won outright. Baldwin favoured giving Labour a chance to experience the trials of office and this came to pass. Today, his head would be on a charger for losing an election so soon after entering No. 10, but Baldwin had made his mark on his party and the country. Even as a rather indifferent Leader of the Opposition he survived, and in little more than a year the Conservatives were back in office with a big majority and a mandate to govern from 1924 until 1929.

Baldwin's background, the family business in iron and steel, gave him a clear understanding of the ills sapping this country's strength. Industrial unrest, mistrust between employers and employees and the consequent strikes were the worst of them. The need for better industrial relations would be Baldwin's theme throughout his political life. At a meeting in Birmingham town hall early in 1925 he said, 'I want a truce of God in this country, that we may compose our differences, that we may join all our strengths together to see if we cannot pull the country into a better and happier condition.' Another passage ran, 'The organizations of employers and men, if they take their coats off to it, are far more able to work out the solutions of their troubles than the politicians. Let them put the State out of their minds and get down to it.' There should be an end once and for all, he urged, to that secretiveness in business 'which has so often poisoned the atmosphere by causing suspicion'.

A test of his thinking came a day or two later in the House of Commons, where a Tory MP named Macquisten was promoting a Private Member's Bill to remove the trade union levy. It was considered unjust that a trade unionist who might be Liberal or Conservative should have to contribute to the funds of the Labour party. The Cabinet was divided on the issue. Baldwin decided to oppose the bill, and did so in a memorable speech.

> I want my Party to-day to make a gesture to the country . . . and to say to them: We have our majority; we believe in the justice of this Bill . . . but we are going to withdraw our hand, we are not going to push our political advantage home . . . Suspicion, which has prevented stability in Europe, is the one poison that is preventing stability at home . . . We, at any rate, are not going to fire the first shot . . . we believe we know what the country wants, and we believe it is for us in our strength to do what no other Party can do, and to say that we at any rate stand for peace.

He closed with the words: 'Although I know that there are those who work for different ends from most of us in this House, yet there are many in all ranks and all parties who will re-echo my prayer: "Give peace in our time, O Lord."' There was, as G. M. Young recognized, a touch of Lincoln in that speech. 'With one stroke,' Young observed, 'he had quelled his dissidents, mastered his Cabinet and projected on Parliament and the country the picture of himself as the kindly reasonable head of the national family.' But the truth, alas, lay closer to what a Labour MP, tears streaming down his face, said to him afterwards: 'It was true, Prime Minister, every word was true. But those times have gone.'

So it appeared, as strife in the coalfields spread and Britain moved towards the General Strike. There is a strange contrast between Baldwin's conduct before and after that event. He had anticipated it and was ready. In 1925, when we were not ready, he had bought off the miners with a subsidy, but by 1926 he had made his dispositions. Churchill was sent off to produce the only newspaper that appeared during the strike, the *British Gazette*, from the old *Morning Post* building in Aldwych, and relished the task – 'interfering with every process' – the old hands recalled when I joined the *Morning Post* a few years later.

The stuff of revolution was lacking in the General Strike. Within a few days it was declared illegal by Mr Justice Astbury and on 12 May, only six days after Baldwin had broadcast a message declaring that 'Constitutional Government is being attacked', the strike was over. Baldwin was hailed as a great national leader, and overseas the strike was misread as a revolutionary challenge which had been seen off by an accomplished statesman. But the coal mines remained in disarray and Baldwin, exhausted by his exertions, subsided into inactivity. 'The Baldwin of 1926,' Tom Jones wrote of him in the *Dictionary of National Biography*, 'stood on a moral level to which it has been doubted that he ever returned. He might have done anything. He did nothing. And ever after he seemed to be trading on an accumulated fund of confidence which was never replenished.'

Here we come to the most difficult part of any analysis of

Stanley Baldwin. He had his moments of inspiration and of political triumph, after which he sometimes lapsed into lethargy and allowed things to go awry. Was it weakness of character, of temperament or physique? Churchill, after all, had moments of inspiration during the Second World War, but never afforded himself the luxury of lethargy. He kept going, constantly under greater stress than Baldwin ever experienced, until the end. Even then, he was strong enough to write his war memoirs, face five years in opposition and then return at the head of a peacetime government. It is a fact that Baldwin's moments of inspiration and triumphs often left him drained and incapable of further effort. Tommy Dugdale, later Lord Crathorne, who was Baldwin's parliamentary private secretary during his final years at Westminster, once told me this story about him.

Baldwin had to address a gathering of Commonwealth ex-servicemen in Westminster Hall just before he retired from Parliament in May 1935. He told them of his sensation on entering the hall of having to brush past the ghosts of those who had fallen in the Great War. It was a short but profoundly moving speech. When it was over, Tommy Dugdale took him back to the Commons smoke room. Baldwin sat down and told the waiter to bring him several glasses of sherry in a tumbler. Knowing that Baldwin was no tippler, Dugdale concluded that he was close to emotional collapse. It was as if he had suffered a haemorrhage, he told me later, and this seems to have happened to Baldwin after great emotional exertions. Baldwin felt the need to spend more time on holiday than any Prime Minister would dare to do today, sometimes six weeks at Aix-les-Bains, taking long walks alone or with his friend Joan

Davidson, wife of his chairman, with whom he enjoyed a close platonic friendship.

From Tom Jones's entry in the *DNB* one might suppose that Baldwin had passed his prime in 1926, but heavy battles lay ahead. The future of India exercised his mind. After the Conservatives lost office in 1929, he came under fierce fire from the newspaper proprietors Rothermere (*Daily Mail*) and Beaverbrook (*Daily* and *Sunday Express*). Baldwin once described his long feud with Beaverbrook as a battle for the soul of Bonar Law but in 1930 it was fought round Beaverbrook's obsession with the notion of Empire free trade. Partly for political, partly for personal reasons, the Beaverbrook newspapers launched their assault on Baldwin at a time when his stock was low within his own party, while Baldwin's quarrel with Rothermere arose partly from the *Daily Mail*'s aversion to self-government for India and from the arrogance of its proprietor. In settling scores with both men Baldwin showed that he had a sharper tongue than admirers of his homely talks supposed. 'I am all for peace,' he said. 'I like the other man to begin the fight, and then I am ready. When I fight I go on to the end, as I did in 1926.'

The crux came with a by-election in the safe Conservative seat of St George's, then one of Westminster's constituencies. It came shortly after the 1929 election had gone to Labour when Baldwin's leadership hung in the balance and one or two of his colleagues were advising him to go. Sir Ernest Petter, a friend of Lord Beaverbrook, stood as an anti-Baldwin candidate. Alfred Duff Cooper, hastening back from a lecture tour overseas and surrendering his safe candidature at Winchester, stood in Baldwin's interests. Mrs Baldwin's diary entries reveal the atmosphere: 'The St George's election causes great excitement.' 'Gutter press throwing mud.' 'Things are getting difficult: I wonder how much more one can bear.'

If you are going to put political opponents down, do it in style. Ignoring the custom that party leaders do not speak at by-elections, Baldwin went to the Queen's Hall during the campaign and let fly. He owed to his cousin Rudyard Kipling the words he used of Rothermere and Beaverbrook, and they have echoed down the years. 'What the proprietorship of these papers is aiming at is power, and power without responsibility, the prerogative of the harlot throughout the ages.' Duff Cooper was returned with a majority of nearly 6,000. As Baldwin wrote to his aunt Edith, 'I thoroughly enjoyed hitting those two rascals and it has done a lot of good.' He always called 1930 'the year my party tried to get rid of me'.

This was petty stuff compared with the crisis that was looming for Britain, where by 1931 the Great Depression was overwhelming Ramsay MacDonald's Labour government. When Labour took office in 1929, the unemployed numbered 1,100,000; early in 1931 the figure was 2,624,000. Baldwin's summer holiday in Aix was interrupted. Summoned back to London on 11 August, he offered MacDonald his political support and returned to Aix. On 20 August Baldwin was again called back to London, was loudly cheered by an anxious crowd at Victoria station, and found himself called upon to serve in a National Government under MacDonald. Some Conservative leaders might have jibbed at this. Baldwin was content to become Lord President of the Council and return to office without the burden of being in charge. Only MacDonald, Philip Snowden (who had been Labour's Chancellor of the Exchequer) and Jimmy Thomas joined the new administration from Labour's ranks. Among the Liberals only Sir John Simon and Sir Herbert Samuel were of the first rank. So MacDonald took charge of a predominantly Conservative administration which in an autumn general election was swept into power with a huge majority by an apprehensive electorate.

Three topics dominated the political agenda: unemployment caused by the collapse of our basic industries such as coal mining, cotton and shipbuilding, self-government for India and rearmament. Early in my life as a reporter on the *Morning Post* I was sent to report the fierce demonstrations of the unemployed round Westminster. The mood struck me as ugly; in reality it was desperate. I have discussed Baldwin's dilemma on rearmament above. On India, he was determined to move forward and a sharp division occurred in the ranks of the Tory party. The *Morning Post* supported Winston Churchill and a minority of Tory party diehards who strenuously opposed the end of British rule in India. Some Conservative MPs supported Churchill while their local associations backed Baldwin, who took the view that we had been pledged to the development of self-government in India since 1919. Some local associations opposed Baldwin while their MPs attacked Churchill. I travelled round the country investigating these differences, which the *Morning Post* gleefully reported. In the end Baldwin had his way; Sir Samuel Hoare, ably assisted by the then promising R. A. Butler as parliamentary under-secretary for India, steered the gigantic Government of India Bill through Parliament. The Second World War postponed the granting of self-government to India, which was ultimately promulgated by Clem Attlee's Labour Government. True, India was the cornerstone of the Empire, and when it was knocked away our imperial days were numbered, but the

Second World War made that process inevitable anyway. G. M. Young once put it to Baldwin that he, MacDonald and Neville Chamberlain must have felt safer with Churchill inside the Cabinet, and asked what kept him out! 'India,' Baldwin replied. 'He had gone about threatening to smash the Tory party on India and I did not mean to be smashed.' Baldwin has never received his due as a principal architect of modern India.

I have come to see 1935 as the fateful year. Mussolini invaded Abyssinia and demonstrated to the world that an aggressor could count on a safe passage from the peace-loving world. The Foreign Secretary Sir Samuel Hoare blundered into an ill-starred agreement with Pierre Laval of France for a peace settlement with Italy which handed the aggressor a hefty slice of Abyssinia, and had to resign. Hitler had established his grip on Germany and would within months reoccupy the Rhineland. It was the year of the League of Nations peace ballot, which countered, indeed prevailed over, the feeling among officials that we must henceforth take rearmament more seriously. The general election which came in the autumn was when rearmament might have been put to the electors but, for the reasons I gave earlier, it was not. MacDonald left No. 10 and Baldwin took over the helm. And to add to this, though the nation was unaware of it, the life of King George V was ebbing away.

The King died in January 1936. Baldwin probably had a clearer idea than anyone else of the difficulties that might lie ahead, but as he put it in his broadcast, 'All eyes are upon him [the Prince of Wales] as he advances to his father's place, and, while he is no stranger to public duty, he is now summoned to face responsibilities more onerous, more exacting, more continuous, than any he has hitherto been asked to discharge.' When George V was seriously ill in 1928, the Prince was urgently recalled from east Africa and Baldwin met him at Folkestone with a warning that he might well have to take over more of his father's duties. The Prince said to Baldwin, 'Now you do understand, don't you, that you can always talk to me about everything.' Baldwin felt moved to reply, 'Sir, I shall remind you of that.'

At his accession, the new King arranged for Mrs Simpson to witness his proclamation from St James's Palace. Then, when he took his summer cruise in the chartered yacht *Nahlin*, she joined him; this was photographed and noticed, though without comment. There were other reasons for disquiet. Old hands found the new regime difficult to stomach, including Lord Wigram, the late King's private secretary, who intimated a wish to resign. Edward was a strong exponent of the cause of Anglo-German understanding, Mrs Simpson even more so. The German embassy in London, where Ribbentrop was ambassador, courted her. While the British press remained silent about the King's association with Mrs Simpson the press overseas showed no such restraint. I was invited by my editor, H. A. Gwynne, to make a collection of foreign press cuttings. Gwynne was close to Baldwin and thought he should see the extent of the interest overseas. Baldwin indicated that he needed more time to consult the King, his own ministers and the Commonwealth.

Early and mid-1936 was a low time for Baldwin. In April he was tested by a vote of confidence in the Commons, where he gave every appearance of losing his grip. A bad Budget leak, leading to the disgrace of his National Government Labour colleague Jimmy Thomas, depressed him. By midsummer he was worn out. In July his doctor, Lord Dawson of Penn, told him to take three months of enforced rest. This was as well, for when he returned to action in October the King's affair with Mrs Simpson had progressed to a critical point. Her divorce, which cited her husband as the guilty party, went through at Ipswich that month and was briefly reported in one or two newspapers. When Baldwin saw the King to discuss the matter on 20 October, he found the King's mind fixed on marriage. At the *Morning Post* I sensed that matters would not long remain out of the public domain and in November urged that we were the most suitable newspaper to break the story. With this in mind Gwynne, doyen of the London press, wrote to Baldwin on 13 November seeking guidance. The newspapers, he pointed out, were finding it difficult to maintain their self-imposed censorship, but if they felt ministers had the matter in hand, they would maintain their silence.

On 16 November, the King, on the advice of his private secretary, summoned Baldwin, who made it clear that marriage to Mrs Simpson would not be approved. The King replied, 'I mean to marry her and I am prepared to go.' Thus, notwithstanding ingenious suggestions for a morganatic marriage, the wheel turned gradually towards abdication. The Dominions were consulted. The political parties held council. The press held to its silence. But everyone reckoned without the Bishop of Bradford, who in course of an otherwise innocent address made an allusion to the King which was interpreted as comment on his affair with Mrs Simpson. The *Yorkshire Post* reported the speech and broke the long silence. On 3 December, the national press were in full cry.

Baldwin saw the King again and told him that the

morganatic proposal was not acceptable. His whips had told him the Conservatives MPs were against it and Attlee reckoned the Labour party would take a similar line. The Dominions returned the same feelings. 'I have known that all along,' the King told Baldwin. There remained Churchill to reckon with, for around him – and Lord Beaverbrook, on the warpath against Baldwin – there briefly appeared the shadow of a King's party. But when so minded, Baldwin could quietly indicate who was in charge. When the King expressed a wish to deliver a broadcast to the Empire, Baldwin expressed his doubts. 'You want me to go, don't you?' the King said. 'And before I go I think it is right, for her sake and mine, that I should speak.' 'What I want, sir,' said Baldwin, 'is what you told me you wanted: to go with dignity, not dividing the country, and making things as smooth as possible for your successor.'

It was not quite the end. Those who disliked Baldwin felt it incumbent upon them to put in a word for the King. 'Give him more time,' was the call. The Conservative 1922 Committee, meeting on 3 December, showed that the parliamentary party was having trouble making up its mind. Baldwin told them to cancel their weekend engagements, go into the pubs and clubs of their constituencies, and to meet again on the following Monday. By then, 7 December, they were of one mind. Churchill was shouted down in the House. Three days later, Baldwin gave the House of Commons an account of his stewardship and the King left the country. 'Whoever writes about the Abdication,' Baldwin told G. M. Young, 'must give the King his due. He could not have behaved better than he did.'

It had not been, as some including Churchill chose to see it, a struggle between the King and his Prime Minister, but rather a struggle by King and Prime Minister to resolve the matter with least damage to the country. Like most of his speeches Baldwin's account to the Commons had been hurriedly jotted down on scraps of paper, and when he reached the front bench he patted his pockets and confessed to his parliamentary private secretary Tommy Dugdale that he had mislaid his notes. Dugdale hastened back to No. 10 and followed a trail of paper up the staircase back to the lavatory. The speech was one of Baldwin's better efforts: lucid, generous and designed to heal wounds. For a time, however, both Baldwin and the Archbishop of Canterbury were seen in some quarters as having cunningly and unjustly pushed the King off his throne. There was talk of the King having upset the government on his recent tour of the Welsh valleys by declaring, 'Something must be done . . .' Ministers, it was declared rather nonsensically, had then determined to get rid of him.

Such feelings did not last, and as the years went by and books about Edward VIII were published, the country came to see that Baldwin's handling of the affair had led to the right result. The Prime Minister had acted on political instinct, with which he was well endowed, and with resolution, on which his record is patchy. He had shown resolution in breaking Lloyd George's hold on his party, in seeking protection for this country's industries during but not after the General Strike, after hesitation in the affray with Rothermere and Beaverbrook and over the King's affair. He failed, however, some historians insist, to gird the country against Hitler's designs.

The abdication was not quite his final duty. That came a little later, as the new King and Queen awaited crowning in Westminster Abbey in May 1937, the month Baldwin gave way to Neville Chamberlain. The coronation was on 12 May.

Early in May a serious dispute in the coal mines was threatened at Haworth colliery in Yorkshire. Attlee sought a debate in the House on the issue, which was granted, and Baldwin decided to speak, while directing Tommy Dugdale, 'we will not inform the colleagues.' He was not long into his speech before those of us listening to him realized that this was his swansong, for it rehearsed the beliefs he had held all his life about peace in industry. His final words were delivered in a stillness I have never known since in the House of Commons:

> In the Abbey on this day week our young King and Queen, who were called suddenly and unexpectedly to the most tremendous position on earth, will kneel and dedicate themselves to the service of their people, a service which can only be ended by death. I appeal to that handful of men with whom rests peace or war to give the best present to the country that could be given at that moment, to do the one thing that would rejoice the hearts of all the people that love this country, that is, to rend and dissipate this dark cloud which has gathered over us, and show the people of the world that this democracy can still at least practise the arts of peace in a world of strife.

I saw Emanuel Shinwell, who was due to follow Baldwin, tear up the notes of his speech.

The debate ended and the House of Commons adjourned. On the night of the coronation itself Baldwin made a short broadcast from London, a performance that caused the BBC anxious moments for he arrived with only the roughest idea of what he proposed to say. It ended with a faint echo of the General Thanksgiving:

> Let us dedicate ourselves – let us dedicate ourselves afresh,

> if need be – to the service of our fellows, a service in widening circles, service to the home, service to our neighbourhood, to our county, our province, to our country, to the Empire, and to the world. No mere service of our lips, service of our lives, as we know will be the service of our King and Queen. God bless them.

To the end and in his seventieth year, Baldwin showed his mastery of the English language. It lay beyond him to order peace in the world, but conscious of what might lie ahead of us, he strove to win peace within the land. So when the time came, we were insufficiently armed but we were one people and resolved. I think it fair to say that was Baldwin's legacy.

Roger Bannister

TO BE AT TWENTY-FIVE the first man in the world to run the mile in a fraction under four minutes is a test of character. The world wants to shake you by the hand. It wants to see you run again soon, and faster if possible, against foreign challengers. It waves opportunities in your face, not all of them useful and some positively deadly. Publishers want a quick book. Television clamours for appearances, but always on their terms not yours. Roger Bannister was fortunate in that at the age of twelve he was seized with a determination to enter and succeed in the medical profession. Then for a while his talent as a runner and his ambition to reach the top of the medical ladder ran in tandem, preserving him from most of the traps that lurk for athletic heroes. In the heady days that followed Bannister's record in 1954, only a trip to America came off the wheels; and because it is a tale of those times, and tells us something about Bannister as a young man, the episode is worth recalling.

The Foreign Office wanted Bannister to make a trip to America. They thought it would improve Anglo-American relations and show the United States what Britain could do. Back in 1954 we were still trying to convince the world that the depredations of the Second World War hadn't written us off. The American television programme *I've Got a Secret* was to be the centrepiece of this endeavour, but other television and radio productions also seemed eager to feature Bannister. British Information Services in New York busied itself with the arrangements. Only after Bannister had reached America was it appreciated that any appearance on commercial television, even if the fees went to charity, could be considered a violation of his amateur status. There was no equivalent of the BBC in America. The International Amateur Athletic Federation spoke darkly of the consequences that might flow from Bannister's appearance on sponsored TV. He was required by the same token to refuse a 'Miracle Mile Trophy' of gold valued at £178. 'Nothing over £12,' stipulated the IAAF.

From this near-fiasco Bannister emerged unscathed. America gave him what was said to be its biggest reception since General MacArthur's return from Korea. 'The Foreign Office has made a perfect fool of itself,' growled the *Daily Herald*. The *Daily Telegraph* commented acidly, 'To send him for the purpose of showing that a Briton could still stand up was superfluous and silly.' But John Russell, director of BIS in New York and later our ambassador in Rio de Janeiro and Madrid, generously observed, 'Roger Bannister is a better diplomat than I am.'

It was the year that shaped the rest of Bannister's life. On 6 May 1954 he ran the mile in 3 minutes 59.4 seconds on the old Iffley Road track at Oxford, a record that stood for just forty-six days and has been surpassed by an average of a third of a second every year since. In July of that same year Bannister passed the last of his examinations, qualified as a doctor at St Mary's Hospital Paddington, and at the close of 1954 announced that he was quitting world-class running. He went on to become a consultant neurologist to two major hospitals and, under the terms of Lord Brain's will, assumed responsibility for the textbook on clinical neurology Brain produced which is now *Brain and Bannister's Clinical Neurology.* There were six editions between 1964 and 1992. Every three or four years Bannister brings it up to date – which he enjoys doing because it keeps *him* up to date. He also treasures the task because, as he once put it to me, 'I wish to be remembered more for my contribution to the medical field than my contribution to sport.'

Bannister's special research interest has been the autonomic system which, he told me, 'you have probably not heard of, but it regulates the heart and circulation. These are functions of the brain which it probably thought wise to exclude from voluntary control. Are you with me? We don't want to know what our heart is doing, we don't want to know whether we are breathing or not . . . this part of the brain does it all for us. How it does it is explained in a book you won't read – it costs a hundred and twenty pounds – but is in continuous demand in libraries.'

I first came to know Roger Bannister when we both served on the Ministry of Health's Advisory Committee on Drug Dependence in the late 1960s. I was there simply as a politician who for a while answered for his party in Parliament on the misuse of dangerous drugs. Roger was there mainly because throughout his adult life he has seemed unable to refuse any chore in the realm of human affairs. Look him up in *Who's Who* and you will find some thirty of these appointments listed before you come to his athletic achievements. Most of them, but by no means all, have been in the field of medicine. Roger was on the Sports Council for some years and was its chairman from 1971 to 1974. He was Master of Pembroke for seven years. He has served and still serves on a wide variety of public bodies. It strikes one as an odd life for someone who set himself to reach the heights in medicine. 'I've always loved doing several things,' he says. Perhaps the Oxford of half a century ago encouraged its sons to spread their talents generously. Bannister is seized with the importance of politics. At Oxford he knew it was not for him, 'but I have been continually drawn back into matters of political importance – the National Health Service, sport, salaries of university staff . . . all this is politics.'

From his earliest days Bannister displayed an independent mind, even on running middle distances. His ideas on how a runner should train aroused controversy. In 1947, on the eve of his eighteenth birthday he won the mile for Oxford. Next year being Olympic year, he was notified that he was seen as an Olympic possible. No, said Bannister, he did not wish to be considered; he thought he was too young. As a medical student he needed no guidance on the runner's physiological problems, doing research into the control of breathing and acting as his own guinea pig. He ascribed his success to the length of his legs – an inside measurement of 35 inches – and to his capacity for absorbing nearly five litres of oxygen a minute. This is about 50 per cent above the normal. It meant he could run up a gradient of one in seven for nine minutes without becoming exhausted.

Essentially, Bannister further explained to me, muscles contain two sorts of fibre: fast-twitch and slow-twitch fibres. 'And we have a mixture of them and that's genetic,' he said. 'But you can, by training, alter the balance of some of the intermediate fibres, make more fast ones or more slow ones, according to the training you do. So sprinters have more fast-twitch fibres and concentrate on developing them. Distance runners have more slow-twitch fibres. And obviously I was born with more slow-twitch fibres and the whole of my training was developing those fibres.'

There is also a psychological side to all this. To Bannister there seemed to be myths about breaking the four-minute barrier. Common sense and physiology, he told me when we met at Oxford, said there was no physical reason why it could not be done. 'It didn't make sense.' He chose the traditional match between Oxford University and the Amateur Athletic Association for an attempt to prove his point. To avoid exciting the press and adding to the tension, Bannister confided his intentions only to a few friends. Among them were the McWhirter twins Norris and Ross, both former Oxford sprinters, and Peter Dimmock, BBC head of sport, who dispatched a cameraman. The key figures in the race itself were Chris Chataway and Chris Brasher, Bannister's pacemakers.

The day began unpromisingly, with wind and rain. Bannister spent part of the morning sharpening his spikes, then took the train from London to Oxford and on the platform at Paddington encountered Franz Stampfl, the Austrian athletics coach. 'Roger,' said Stampfl, 'if you have the chance and don't take it, you may never forgive yourself. Sure it'll be painful, but what's pain?' Stampfl was a man to whom people paid attention. Interned as an Austrian by the British at the start of the Second World War, he was sent to Canada in a ship that was torpedoed. Most of the passengers drowned. Stampfl was eight hours in the sea before being rescued.

History records that Bannister's lunch on that day was an omelette with lettuce and tomato salad, prunes and custard and nothing to drink. Bannister called on Chataway. 'The forecast says the wind may drop towards evening,' said Chataway. 'Let's not decide until five o'clock.' The wind did drop. From the Iffley Road track Bannister saw the St George's flag on a nearby church begin to droop. There was a false start, for which Brasher apologized, then the gun fired for the second time.

Bannister described the race in the book he wrote about his early life, *The First Four Minutes*. 'Brasher went into the lead and I slipped in effortlessly behind him, feeling tremendously full of running. My legs seemed to meet no resistance at all, as if propelled by some unknown force.' Reckoning the pace too slow, Bannister called to Brasher to go faster. In fact Brasher ran the first two laps in exactly the right time, 1 minute 58 seconds for the half-mile. Then, as he tired, Chataway took over for the third and fourth laps and took Bannister to 240 yards from the finish. It was Bannister's ability to sustain a sprint over the last 200 yards that separated him from his contemporaries. His split times were 57.5, 60.7, 62.3 and 58.9 seconds. Three separate timekeepers had to agree.

The announcement was delivered by Norris McWhirter, author of the *Guinness Book of Records*. 'Ladies and Gentlemen, here is the result of Event number nine, the one mile. First, number forty-one Roger Bannister of the AAA and formerly of Exeter and Merton Colleges, with a time which is a new meeting and track record and which, subject to ratification, will be the new English native, British national and British all-comers', European, British Empire and world record. The time is three—' The rest of his announcement was lost in an explosion of applause. 'It was only then,' Bannister recorded later, 'that real pain overtook me. I felt like an exploded flashlight with no will to live. I just went on existing in the most passive physical state without being unconscious.' But he recovered well enough to go to Walter Morris, the Iffley Road groundsman, and thank him for getting the track in good shape. Who can tell what would have happened if the wind had not suddenly dropped on that evening of 6 May? It would have made a difference of about one second a lap, Bannister told me recently, so he would have to have done the mile in 3 minutes 56 seconds. And after that? Within sixty-two days of his mile record he had qualified as a doctor and was leading a disciplined life at St Mary's Hospital. Bannister's mile reminds us of life's fleeting chances.

Born in 1929, he was the first member of his family to go to university. He first approached Cambridge, who asked him to wait a year; Oxford offered to take him at once. His father was a junior civil servant and a Methodist, his mother a Sunday-school teacher and Unitarian. After the family moved from Harrow to Bath at the start of the Second World War, Bannister went to the local grammar school. He was what we would now call a workaholic. 'You'll be dead before you're twenty-one if you go on at this rate,' a master told him. All his life Roger Bannister has been the sort of person who sets targets in life and then works tenaciously towards achieving them. But this attitude does not always attract close friendships at school. So he struck a lonely figure at Oxford among the war veterans and his contemporaries with public school backgrounds. There was nothing remarkable in wanting to be a doctor; running was his passport to recognition. In those days politics was highly thought of at Oxford. Remembering something of them, I know Bannister is right when he says a shade wistfully, 'When I was at Oxford in 1946, politics was regarded as possibly the finest career . . . demanding intelligence, ability and a willingness to take risks.' He knew it was not for him, 'but quite a large part of me would have liked to go into politics'.

Bannister's renown as an athlete tends to obscure his main achievement. When the Second World War ended and he first went to Oxford, a number of fresh ideals were gradually forming. There was an awareness, looking back on the 1930s, that certain things would have to change. The old ways, as President John Kennedy later expressed it, would not do any more. The society with which we had entered the Second World War had had its virtues, but it did not fit the aspirations of young men and women in the post-war world. For a generation that had spent five years at war, social patterns had changed: there had to be more regard for merit, less weight attached to birth. I remember an uncomfortable talk with Sir William Haley, who had moved from being Director General of the BBC to the editor's chair at *The Times*. The Tory party, he informed me sharply, had lost its way; it was still the party of privilege. The future, he insisted, lay in creating a meritocracy, where men and women were rewarded for what they did rather than for what they were. He eyed me accusingly. Having earned my living as a journalist from the age of eighteen, I felt slightly miffed, but the old so-and-so was right. Meritocracy was on its way. The City of London today could not do its work without it. It has spread through the professions and will be found occupying the best of London clubs. Bannister himself is a shining example of it.

I cottoned on to this while we were talking at Oxford and expressed anxiety about the future of his profession which, I suggested to him, the National Health Service has turned into something like a treadmill. Given such conditions, would it continue to attract the best talents? 'Very able people,' he insisted, 'are attracted to a profession which is a meritocracy; where they will have their skills and hard work justified.' But were we not, I countered, propping up our NHS by importing doctors and nurses from countries which needed them more than we do? 'About one in three of those wanting to train in medicine,' replied Roger, 'are from the Asian community, knowing it is a meritocracy, knowing it is a stable career and a salaried profession.' If we accept what he says, then the meritocracy which he himself illustrates has drawn talent to Britain that our society would otherwise lack.

A man who depends entirely on his own efforts to climb as high as Bannister has needs a moderating influence in his life. He found it in Moyra Jacobsson, daughter of a former head of the International Monetary Fund. Their children, says Bannister, explaining their success in life, have inherited her genes. Moyra is an artist. Looking at some of her paintings on the walls of their Oxford home, I sensed the sort of influence she has had on the life of a man who feels he must be perpetually on the go. He is less didactic than most experts, whether talking of drugs or sport or exercise. Who can reasonably quarrel with these observations?

'To be effective, exercise should become a habit, and like other habits, is best learnt in childhood. That is why the drastic decline in school sports programmes as well as the selling of school sports facilities is scandalous . . . Education authorities cannot have understood the deleterious effect of these policies'.

'Some children do find competitive sport difficult. But even if pupils lack the skills to succeed in sport, life itself brings reverses. Sport is a way of learning to accept them with grace.'

Bannister had a bad car accident in 1975 which damaged bones in his ankle, but it didn't slow him up for long. I was glad to hear that at the age of seventy-three he plays golf twice a week. The habit of climbing the long ladder to success without pausing for breath is hard to break at any age. For there is always another rung.

William Berry, 1st Viscount Camrose

PLACE HAD TO BE found for a newspaperman of my times in this collection – but which one? The most acquisitive, and some would say the most successful, is Rupert Murdoch, whom I first came to know in his native Australia. The most colourful is the Canadian Max Beaverbrook, whose *Daily Express* was so strikingly successful in the early 1930s. I met him only once, at a grand dinner given to mark his eighty-fifth birthday in 1964, a short time before he died. A lesser known but by no means uninfluential figure is William Berry, Viscount Camrose, who acquired the *Daily Telegraph* in 1928 and remained its proprietor and editor-in-chief until his death in 1954. I have chosen him not simply because he was my boss for some years but because of the good example he set in a rough and highly competitive business.

WILLIAM BERRY

Starting life with nothing, William Berry built up a vast publishing business. He became, as his son Michael Hartwell described him in his biography, a 'giant of Fleet Street', an outstanding self-made man of the twentieth century. All three sons of Alderman Mathias Berry of Merthyr Tydfil and his wife Mary Ann were raised to the peerage. I came to admire William Berry for his modesty which some mistook for shyness, his skills as a newspaperman and his political judgement – though, unlike Beaverbrook, he appeared to have no political ambitions for himself. I also found his dry sense of humour attractive.

Soon after I rejoined the *Daily Telegraph* in 1945 and was put to work on the Peterborough column, Hugo Wortham, who ran the column, was invited to one of Camrose's small staff lunches and was asked to bring me along with him. Wortham was an irascible Edwardian with a warm heart, well versed in literature and the arts, and a wine buff. As six or eight of us sat at our proprietor's lunch table, jugs of claret appeared, the necks of which were faintly misty. 'My God,' exclaimed Wortham in the sudden silence that sometimes falls before someone drops a clanger, 'they've boiled the claret again!' Nothing was said at the time, but some weeks later we were invited to another lunch. Choosing his moment, Camrose remarked drily as the wine went round, 'I trust this claret meets with your approval, Mr Wortham.'

I have several reasons for feeling grateful towards Camrose. After he bought and incorporated the ailing *Morning Post* into the *Telegraph* in 1937, most of the *Post*'s staff were pensioned off, but a handful of us were brought into the *Daily Telegraph*. As the *Post*'s political correspondent, I had been earning an excellent salary of £750 a year with an expense account of

£250, on top of which normal expenses could be charged. They ran a tight ship at the *Telegraph* and when I got there the post of political correspondent was already occupied, but Camrose authorized my old salary and allowance, though I would have been grateful for a job there at any price. After the war, when I rashly put myself forward as prospective Conservative candidate for the Ashford division in Kent, he sent me a note of encouragement, wishing me well and a seat in the Cabinet. Not many employers would take that line with political aspirants on their staff these days.

One of William Berry's strengths was that he had had a more thorough grounding in journalism than most of us. He began his working life at the age of fourteen as a cub journalist on the *Merthyr Times*. At eighteen he moved to London and became a reporter on the *Investors' Guardian* at thirty-five shillings a week. He lost that job, suffered three months of unemployment – something he never subsequently forgot in dealings with his staff – then got back to work as a reporter with the Commercial Press Association. The foundations of his empire were laid in 1901 when he decided to launch a paper of his own, *Advertising World*. He set it up with £100 borrowed from his elder brother Seymour Barry, later Lord Buckland, whose business was in Welsh coal and steel. Single-handed, as editor, subeditor, canvasser for advertising, copy writer and layout man, he wrote every word of the first issue. His younger brother Gomer Berry, later Lord Kemsley, joined him to look after the business side. By 1904 *Advertising World* had taken off and the Berry brothers began to look around with a discerning eye for other publications. One of them was *Boxing*, a sport which William was enthusiastic about; he also had an eye on *Health & Strength*, a periodical devoted to physical culture, which was catching on in Britain. He acquired it in 1906. The message it delivered was stark:

> Eighty per cent of the ailments people suffer from are the direct outcome of rank stupidity . . . The case of Mr Chamberlain is a striking example. For years Mr Chamberlain was cited as an instance of what a man could do without exercise of any kind. During all the stress and strain of the Boer War Mr Chamberlain's only exercise was the absolutely necessary walk within the walls of Government buildings. His pitiful and absolute physical collapse is a matter of history . . . Mr Gladstone was hale and vigorous to the end of his days. *Health & Strength* is for everyone who believes in being 'fit' as opposed to an ailing whining liverish state.

The magazine acquired a young Danish physical training expert, Jorgen Muller. William took him on a lecture tour of the industrial north and Midlands. Muller showed off his methods; *Health & Safety* flourished. In 1909 William sold *Advertising World* for £11,000 and the brothers moved to houses in the country. At thirty-five, married and with five children, he was above the age for army service in 1914. By the time the age limit was lifted he had suffered an attack of peritonitis which nearly killed him and he was listed as Category C, exempt from military service due to his being a newspaper editor. Thus in 1915 he was in a position to make his first big move and purchase the *Sunday Times.* That sounds a big deal now, but the *Sunday Times* was not what it is today; it sold about 50,000 copies against the *Observer*'s 200,000 while the *Sunday Telegraph* did not yet exist. William presided over the *Sunday Times* as editor-in-chief for twenty-two years. By 1949 it was selling 568,000 copies against the *Observer*'s 384,000.

A year after the Great War, the Berry brothers acquired

Clements Press and with it the *Financial Times.* Kelly's Directories, Weldon's Group and Graphic Publications were subsequently added to their holdings. In 1921 William was created a baronet without, his son Michael Hartwell assures us, a penny piece going in the direction of Lloyd George, whose sale of honours around that period was notorious.

The next big move, in 1924, was the foundation of Allied Newspapers, controlled by the Berry brothers and Sir Edward Iliffe, later Lord Iliffe. It took over most of the Hulton papers from Lord Rothermere, including big provincial holdings. Two years later the Amalgamated Press, comprising non-political publications, a printing works and a paper mill, was taken over from the executors of Lord Northcliffe. All that was lacking from the empire was a national daily. That final element came in 1927 when Lord Burnham, owner of the *Daily Telegraph*, was appointed to a mission in India. He approached the Berry–Iliffe group with a view to a sale. Lord Rothermere of the *Daily Mail*, travelling in America at the time, was furious to hear news of a further Berry expansion. He felt the Harmsworth dynasty was under attack and threatened fierce competition. In fact, as Michael Hartwell makes plain in his biography, the purchase of the *Daily Telegraph* in December 1927 was 'more of a challenge than an accolade'.

Its circulation was in free fall. Standing at 300,000 before the foundation of the *Daily Mail* in 1896, it had dropped to 180,000 by 1914, to 130,000 in 1920 and at the time of the sale was down to 84,000. *The Times*, on 130,000 and fostered by Northcliffe, had political supremacy and was making money. Having taken the *Telegraph* over, however, William Berry was careful to avoid any suggestion of a revolution. He was able to reassure an apprehensive staff about his intentions, believing that the appearance rather than the content of the newspaper was its principal weakness. A managing editor, Arthur Watson, was put in charge, and was still there when I arrived ten years later. Lord Burnham's nephew Fred Lawson remained as general manager and after the Second World War became managing director. What transformed the newspaper's prospects was William's decision in 1930 to cut its price from 2d to 1d. Circulation doubled in a day to 200,000. The Berry–Iliffe group by this time owned two nationals, six provincial dailies, eight provincial evenings and seventy periodicals. There was no interference with the politics of any of these publications.

William Berry's talent, born of early experience, was knowing how to make newspapers look readable. His subeditor's eye saw that the way news and features were jammed into the *Telegraph* in no set order made the newspaper look unappetizing. He had acquired a newspaper, as his son points out, where the printer was boss. The dictatorship of the printer was common to all newspapers; William's printer at the *Telegraph*, Francis Caine, had once ordered Lord Northcliffe out of his composing room. It took all William's skills allied to tact to get Caine to change his ways without breaking his heart. 'He knew what he wanted,' as Michael Hartwell put it, 'in terms of white space, double-column heads and introductions, heading types and type sizes, cross-heads and the use of photographs.'

Some of the memoranda he sent out show how his mind worked. 'A house is not a mansion nowadays, even when it belongs to the Marquess of Londonderry.' 'Is there any reason to continue the old formula "Lady Cottenham explained what happened to a Press Representative last night?" Obviously it could not have been anyone else.' 'An excellent little story on the antiquity of mint sauce.' 'It is a good idea to have every day a human story on the turn [second news] page.' 'In the story of the French President's marriage it would have been an excellent thing if the subeditor had thought of including the President's age.' 'Is our crime man still on the staff? The news in other papers would appear to indicate he is not.'

With Rothermere and Beaverbrook also in Fleet Street competition was fierce. The 1930s was the era when national newspapers resorted to gift schemes to boost their circulations. Loyal readers of a newspaper could, for example, acquire a set of encyclopedias. William Berry would have none of it. When he bought the *Morning Post* in 1937, shut it down later in the year and for a while ran under the title *Daily Telegraph and Morning Post*, there were hard feelings about the newspaper's demise but I came to see that it was inevitable. It was the social change wrought by the Great War, not William Berry, that killed off the *Morning Post.*

In the year that the *Morning Post* was absorbed, the Berry–Iliffe empire split. Gomer Berry sold his interests in the *Daily Telegraph*, the *Financial Times* and the Amalgamated Press to William. William sold his stake in Allied Newspapers to Gomer and his share of Kelly's Directories to Iliffe.

For what now seems the paltry sum of £320,000 Berry built the new *Telegraph* office, with its handsome clock, which still stands in Fleet Street. This prompted Beaverbrook to erect a gleaming office clad with black glass lower down the hill in order to look top dog, but by 1939 Lord Camrose (as he had become) had raised the circulation of the *Telegraph* to 750,000.

Unlike some of his rivals, Camrose was not a political animal. He favoured Lloyd George for a while until he became repelled by his political opportunism and thought well of

Stanley Baldwin for his desire to bind all classes together. His *Daily Telegraph* was to be in close sympathy with the policy of the Conservative party but ready to express an independent view when circumstances warranted it.

When it came to the abdication of King Edward VIII, Camrose kept a steady hand on the newspaper. He was close to Churchill, who became a contributor to the *Telegraph*, but was not tempted, as Churchill, Beaverbrook and Rothermere were, to back the King against Baldwin. Camrose made it his job to keep closely informed; he saw the principal politicians involved, listened to what they had to say and eventually supported the Prime Minister.

In the *Daily Telegraph's* reporters' room which I joined in 1937 and where I worked partly as a Whitehall correspondent and increasingly as civil defence correspondent writing about air raid precautions, we were slightly in awe of our editor-in-chief but happy to gossip about his small idiosyncrasies. He tended to be fussy about other men's titles in relation to his own. There were also many more public dinners in those days, usually in white ties, many of which Camrose attended primarily to keep himself abreast of what was happening. *Telegraph* reporters at such dinners were expected to approach him at the end of the meal and receive instructions on which speeches to report and how much space to give them. There is a jolly – and true – story about a reporter on a late turn in the newsroom who rang the canteen upstairs and peremptorily ordered a cup of coffee and a ham sandwich. He mistakenly dialled Camrose's house number. The sandwich and coffee arrived. Camrose then rang the reporter to ask if everything was entirely to his satisfaction.

At the *Morning Post* in 1936 we had taken up the words of

King Edward VIII delivered at a steelworks outside Merthyr Tydfil just before his abdication: 'These works brought these men here. Something must be done to put them back to work.' It was decided to raise enough money from our readers to send every child of unemployed parents in the Distressed Areas, of which South Wales was a part, a decent Christmas present anonymously by post. With the help of school teachers and others – and a cheque from the King himself – we made a good job of it and sent presents to 120,000 children. On Christmas Day the news editor and I travelled round the Welsh valleys to see the result of our handiwork. It was a moving scene, because not many presents were going down that way in those years. As luck would have it, it was a mild sunny day and the children were out with their toys.

Soon after I joined the *Telegraph* in 1937, Camrose asked if I would take the appeal on again. I agreed. Some 42,000 responded to our appeal that year and 214,000 children got presents. I ran the appeal during the week and spent Saturdays in the Distressed Areas gathering material to move our readers' hearts. This led to the only minor disagreement I ever had with Arthur Watson. One weekend I planned to visit Merthyr Tydfil again, which had the highest unemployment rate of any British town. Watson was troubled by this. 'It is sensitive territory for the Berry family,' he reasoned with me. In fact only the eldest brother Lord Buckland, who had died after a riding accident, had had his main business there. I thought Watson was doing Camrose an injustice in supposing he would take offence, politely told him so and ran some sobstuff from Merthyr Tydfil about a girl of twelve with a pinched white face whom I watched gazing lovingly into a toy shop window with her little brother. As I anticipated there was no reaction from

Camrose and I felt that I had read his essentially grown-up character more accurately than had his managing editor. Because of the weight of the traffic some of the gifts had to arrive just before Christmas and few children's thank you letters came in from their school teachers. On Christmas Eve, I put them in a satchel and sent them down to Camrose's country home at Hackwood by dispatch rider. Experiences with the Children's Fund left me with warm feelings towards him; I felt his heart was in the right place.

The most testing time I had at the *Telegraph* before the war was around the time of the Munich conference. I was close to Victor Gordon Lennox, our diplomatic correspondent, a resolute opponent of appeasement. Meanwhile, Camrose and his eldest son Seymour, who had become joint managing editor at the *Telegraph*, kept in touch with ministers. The outcome of Chamberlain's three visits to Germany in 1938, culminating in Munich, was generally hailed with profound relief although Camrose's *Telegraph* observed: 'It is never to be forgotten that if a war has been averted a great injustice has been suffered by a small and friendly people and there must be a sense of humiliation that we should have had to urge on that nation such proposals.'

After Munich, Camrose became increasingly critical of Chamberlain who, sensing this, sought through Halifax at the Foreign Office to dissuade him from publishing provocative leaders in the *Telegraph*. Far from obliging, Camrose published a long leader urging Churchill's inclusion in the government. Perhaps it was as well the brothers William and Gomer had divided their interests; while William began to lose confidence in Chamberlain, Gomer's *Sunday Times* remained supportive.

When war came, Camrose spent a few weeks as controller of press relations at the unwieldy Ministry of Information. He reduced the staff by a third, then announced his resignation five weeks after joining. He had nothing more to do with the ministry until four years later when, according to his son's account, Beaverbrook prevented his appointment as minister. He would have liked to have taken command of that ramshackle department and might well have made a good job of it, but it was not to be. However, as the war wore on, Camrose had become increasingly close to Churchill, supportive of him and sensitive – as not everyone was – to the colossal strain the progress of the war was imposing on the Prime Minister.

When the war was over, Camrose took two steps which secured Churchill's post-war future. He wrote to some of his wealthy friends and raised enough money to buy Churchill's home in Kent, Chartwell, for the nation. It provided Churchill in those difficult years with something at his back. He also negotiated a deal whereby the *Daily Telegraph* secured Churchill's war memoirs for serialization. This was done lawfully but in a fashion which saved Churchill a vast amount in taxes. Camrose recouped his outlay with some shrewd syndication of the memoirs to other international publications.

When Camrose died, rather unexpectedly, in 1954, I was a junior minister and subject to orders but I remember telling my private secretary that the service held for him in the crypt of St Paul's Cathedral must take priority over all my other engagements. Harold Nicholson recorded in his diary: 'I see the flags at half-mast in Fleet Street and on the posters that Camrose has died. He was a staunch friend and wise counsellor. He showed that one could be a Press Lord and a gentleman. He was an example to the newspaper world and I am wretched at his death.' So was I.

Rab Butler

THERE WERE TWO OCCASIONS in the life of Richard Austin Butler, KG, CH, better known as Rab, when he came close to being appointed Prime Minister. The first was in 1957, when a breakdown in health and the Suez debacle brought about the sudden retirement of Anthony Eden. The second was in 1963, when Macmillan, after a stressful year, had to undergo an operation on his prostate gland and decided that he could no longer continue as Prime Minister. On that occasion, if Rab had chosen to fight for the premiership, he could well have prevailed. Instead, he decided the right thing to do was to step aside and serve in the administration formed by Alec Douglas-Home.

Because he twice lost the chance of occupying 10 Downing Street, Rab Butler's long career in politics has been seen as a disappointment, a failure even. 'He was most famous for not becoming Prime Minister,' Roy Jenkins has somewhat ironically observed. Furthermore, his reluctance to fight for the job in 1963 has been regarded, even by his admirers, as exemplifying a flaw in his character. When it came to the point, they argued, Rab lacked the steel to stand his ground and win. Add to this today's belief that only first prizes are worth the winning, and the devaluation of public service, and it is not hard to see why Rab, even within his own party, receives less honour than is his due. Yet in reality he left a bigger footprint on the politics of his time than many Conservative Prime Ministers have done. The contribution he made to his party and to this country before, during and after the exacting Second World War was of a high order. He stands among the most influential British politicians of the last century.

I encountered Butler relatively early in his political career. In 1937, the last year of the *Morning Post*'s life, I was the newspaper's political correspondent. It was a great time to be in the lobby of the House of Commons: that year Ramsay MacDonald retired from political life, Neville Chamberlain succeeded Stanley Baldwin and Lloyd George was still there. Churchill was sounding the alarm over the pace of German rearmament and there was a growing realization that the threat from Hitler was serious. But Rab had just taken a sideways step in his career: in May Neville Chamberlain made him junior minister at the Ministry of Labour. He had held the relatively safe Conservative seat of Saffron Walden in Essex since winning it in 1929, and as a very young parliamentary under secretary for India, had won his political spurs by helping Samuel Hoare pilot through Parliament the huge Government of India Bill.

I had admired Rab's handling of the India bill against fierce opposition from Winston Churchill, a contingent of Tory diehards and my own newspaper. 'They've given you a breather,' I said, when we met in the lobby one afternoon. He gave me one of his sideways smiles and drew from his pocket a small booklet entitled *Standing Orders: Ministry of Labour*. To acquaint himself quickly with his new department and find time for everything else, he said gloomily, he was studying the booklet in the lavatory. But the ordeal did not last for long; in February 1938 Chamberlain asked him to go as number two to the Foreign Office. The Foreign Secretary Lord Halifax was in the House of Lords so this was a leap forward as Rab had to answer for the Foreign Office in the Commons. The Spanish Civil War made it an especially hazardous post, for whether or not we should intervene was a contentious issue. Facing up to seventy questions a week, Rab's stonewalling in defence of non-intervention had won Churchill's approval. So when the government came to be reconstructed in May 1940, Churchill told him, 'I wish you to go on with your delicate manner of answering parliamentary questions without giving anything away.' Rab was one of the few staunch supporters of Neville Chamberlain – and thus associated with appeasement – to retain Churchill's confidence. He remained at the Foreign Office under Halifax and then Eden until July 1941 when Churchill sent for him. 'You have been in the House fifteen years and it is time you were promoted.' Butler protested gently that he had been there for only twelve years, but this was waved aside. 'I now want you to go to the Board of

Education. I think you will leave your mark there,' Churchill told him.

It turned out to be a good prophecy. The war itself and constant tinkering with our system of education in recent years have obscured Rab Butler's achievement in making the Education Act of 1944 possible. There had been no major reform of education for forty years but with rare political skill Butler secured the agreement of the churches to comprehensive changes. Every child was given the right to free secondary education. Provision was made for the expansion of nursery and further education and for raising the school-leaving age. After the war, I served on a committee with James Chuter-Ede, who had been parliamentary under secretary to Butler at the Board of Education in the wartime coalition and who later became Labour's Home Secretary. He described to me some of the cliffs they had had to climb in making the 1944 act a reality. Chuter-Ede kept records of all the negotiations and took steps to have these important documents preserved after his death. So Rab enjoyed a successful war on the home front, and emerged from it with an enhanced parliamentary reputation.

Butler was one of the ministers on the committee entrusted with plans for post-war reconstruction. He was also seen to be right in opposing what proved a fatal decision to go for an early general election in July 1945. He thought the coalition government should continue to serve until Japan had been defeated. Butler's experience of pre-war Britain, with its high unemployment and the Distressed Areas – which I had shared – made him less sanguine than some of his colleagues about receiving a grateful response from the electors after victory in Europe. 'The overwhelming electoral defeat of 1945 shook the

Conservative party out of its lethargy and impelled it to re-think its philosophy and re-form its ranks with a thoroughness unmatched for a century,' Rab observed later in his memoirs, *The Art of the Possible*.

Churchill, aged by the war, was unlikely to be found in the vanguard of such a movement, while not all the talents he had gathered together for fighting the war, some of whom remained on his front bench, had their roots in the Tory party. He made the right choice for the party's chairman in Lord Woolton, who had been a popular Minister of Food, but the intellectual muscle and tenacity called for in rethinking the party's philosophy and strategy had to come from someone like Butler. As chairman of the Conservative Research Department and of the party's industrial policy committee, he became architect of a new post-war party.

So there slowly came to life the *Industrial Charter*, which some wag described as an attempt to 'amalgamate the Tory party with the YMCA'. That was not far off the mark, as Butler admitted later, 'for what basically we were saying is that, untouched by morality and idealism, economics is an arid pursuit, just as politics is an unprofitable one'. Churchill accepted the *Industrial Charter* as a statement of policy round which those opposed to the rigid doctrines of socialism could rally. As the political influence of the wartime members of the Cabinet slowly receded, Butler's standing in the party grew stronger. He was good with some of the able young Tory MPs, such as Iain Macleod, Angus Maude and Reggie Maudling, who had emerged from the war with strong ideas but little experience of politics. By 1950, when I first entered the Commons, Rab had been in politics for twenty years, and for most of them he had held ministerial rank. He was the source to which some of us turned for guidance.

So when the tide turned in 1951, returning Churchill to power, Butler was an obvious candidate for the Treasury although in some respects Oliver Lyttelton seemed a more likely choice as he understood the City and was closer to Churchill. However, Lyttelton lacked Butler's mastery of the House of Commons and Rab got the job. It was a testing time for any Chancellor of the Exchequer. The war had left us with a huge overdraft yet people longed to be delivered from the stringencies of the post-war years. Had not the Tories promised to 'Set the People Free'? Rab's first two popular Budgets met requirements sufficiently to be considered successful, but the strain of public life increased. When both Churchill and Eden were sick during 1953, Butler was called on to hold the reins. At the end of 1954 he suffered a personal tragedy: his wife Sydney died after a long illness. It threw him out of his stride. When Eden took over from Churchill in the early summer of 1955, he offered Butler relief from the Treasury, which Rab mistakenly declined.

It was then that his ambiguities, or 'Rabisms', began to make mischief for him. As I came to know Rab, these indiscretions puzzled me until I came to see that at least some of the mischief was woven round them by my profession of journalism. Interviewed by a Press Association reporter at London Airport in December 1955, for example, Rab was asked, 'Mr Butler, would you say that this is the best Prime Minister we have?' It was a daft question, but also a trap. 'Yes,' said Rab. In the way newspapers have, this was converted into a far more damaging direct quotation: 'Eden is the best Prime Minister we have.' Some of the silly things he said came when his mind was elsewhere. This, for example, was how he opened an address in Copenhagen which Alec Douglas-Home had committed the Foreign Secretary to giving: 'Sir Alec Douglas-Home accepted this invitation to address you. I am here in his place. I am honoured to be here. But I wish it could have been him who was here tonight.' The Danish audience fortunately laughed heartily.

There is no denying that some of the remarks fairly attributed to Rab lack the ring of loyalty. Discussing Suez with Nicko Henderson, later our ambassador in Washington, when they were together at the Foreign Office, Rab declared, 'Of course, the party held that against me but I was not disloyal to Eden. I was critical because I thought it mismanaged. Being the son of a civil servant I also thought it wrong to treat officials as Eden did over Suez. I didn't like collusion either. I should have resigned, shouldn't I?' A number of Rabisms bore no malice but were simply incomprehensible. Addressing a waiter at a Lancaster House reception he said, 'Please bring me a glass of whisky with enough water added to make it liquid.'

I was close to Rab early in 1957, after Eden had resigned and Macmillan had been preferred. For my part I had decided that junior office on £1,500 a year with £500 of parliamentary salary added was insufficient to sustain our family of four children and so had retired from office. Rab was sympathetic and we had a quiet lunch together at his house in Smith Square. Churchill had told him, 'I went for the older man,' whatever that meant. Lord Salisbury had advised him: 'It matters less what position you hold than being *in* politics.' He commended this thought to me and took very seriously the lesser positions he held. He became Leader of the House and Home

Secretary. Later, in 1959, he added a third hat and became chairman of the Conservative party. Some were critical of this arrangement, reckoning Rab was bound to muff one of the three major jobs, but he was an experienced administrator and a quick worker. A riding accident at the age of six which broke his right arm in three places had left him with a crippled arm and hand, but he could enter minutes on the papers laid before him quicker than most of his colleagues. 'I never look at my boxes after 1 a.m.,' he assured me once.

No matter how heavy the burdens of office, he was an exemplary Member of Parliament. If you went to stay a week-end with him in Essex and arrived before lunch on Saturday, you would find him on the telephone. He kept a list of people in his Saffron Walden constituency whose opinion he valued and would make random calls to them. People were mildly flattered, at least in those days, to hear their MP on the tele-phone, saying, 'I would greatly value your opinion about . . .' How delightful to be able to say at some dinner party, 'Well, as a matter of fact – and this must go no further – our Member of Parliament sought my advice on this very topic . . .'

While Rab was Foreign Secretary I agreed to speak at a local meeting with him. Cyprus was in crisis. Delayed at the Foreign Office on this account, he arrived later than expected. It seemed reasonable to expect from him some account of his dealings with Cyprus. Oh no. He opened his speech by saying he had been following closely in the Essex newspapers a local bone of contention – I think it was about a public lavatory in some high street. The Foreign Secretary captured more ears on that topic than he would have done on Cyprus. One Saturday night, I remember, we went off before dinner to an unexciting constituency event; if you were a guest at Stanstead Hall, which his father-in-law Samuel Courtauld had given him along with a tax-free income of £5,000 a year, you were expected to accompany the Member of Parliament on his constituency duties.

At the Home Office from 1957 until 1962 Rab discovered, as he put it later, that even for unadventurous spirits the department never provides a rest cure. 'It is residuary legatee of every problem of internal government not specifically assigned to some other department,' he wrote in *The Art of the Possible*, 'and many of these problems are politically sensitive, straddling the controversial borderline between liberty and order.' He was seen as a sensitive Home Secretary, who not only kept the flogging and hanging element in the Conservative party at bay but, more positively, produced the enlightened *Penal Policy in a Changing Society*. Many saw this as a great state paper, offering a more liberal approach to punishment than might have been expected from a Tory Home Secretary. He also found time for occasional jokes. A demonstration outside No. 10 Downing Street had become threatening and the police were called in. A police dog, standing with its handler under the Foreign Office arch opposite, barked threateningly. This was seen as an act of intimidation and infuriated the demonstrators. Questions were asked in the Commons. Files flew round the Home Office. Officials pointed out that the dog had been taken along in all good faith and most unfortunately had barked at the wrong moment and upset the demonstrators. Recognizing a storm in a teacup, Rab entered the minute: 'Who advised the dog?'

With his second marriage in October 1959 to Mollie, widow of Augustine Courtauld, polar explorer and a relative by marriage of his late wife, Rab's private life became happier and his political burdens lighter. He needed someone close to him who could fathom his moods and stop dark thoughts from tempting him into uttering silly and damaging remarks. Though he lost two of his positions in October 1961, retaining only the Home Office, I reckoned he was on a high plane up to March 1962 when Macmillan persuaded him to take charge of a new central Africa department, sweetened with the title of First Secretary of State. Then with the damaging massacre of the Cabinet which followed in July 1962, he was moved from the Home Office and left with the African imbroglio. It spoke well of him that he took over this thankless chore without complaint and set about the apparently hopeless task of peacefully dissolving the Central African Federation.

I had been close enough to that scene to know the extent of the tangle Rab was called on to unravel, and having reluctantly returned to ministerial life and joined the Cabinet in the crisis of July 1962, I had a full view of his dogged persistence on this treadmill. The big crisis for him came when Macmillan's prostate trouble led him to surrender office in October 1963. The Cabinet at that time included several potential successors – Butler, Hailsham, Macleod, Maudling and Alec Douglas-Home. Macmillan at first favoured Hailsham and, I have always thought, said enough to over-excite him. Then, after the Tory conference at Blackpool where confused soundings were taken, Macmillan supported Alec Home. As I was supposed to be in charge of the Government's public appearance in all this, I tried to take a detached view, expressing no opinion of my own, but accepting the majority verdict.

Because the choice of Alec Home was controversial, we kept it quiet until the last moment. It leaked out just in time for a small protest meeting to be called by Butler's adherents at Enoch Powell's home in Eaton Terrace. On being summoned by the Queen, Alec Douglas-Home sensibly proposed seeing if he could form an administration before accepting her commission. If at that point Rab had refused to serve, Home's administration would have been badly holed and probably have sunk. Instead Rab agreed to serve as Foreign Secretary.

There was, as I have written elsewhere, a strong element of service before self in Rab Butler's character. He once recited with approval a curious little ditty which showed how his mind turned on service: 'Nations earn their right to rise by service and by sacrifice.' He and Alec Douglas-Home had been parliamentary colleagues since the 1930s. and Butler had held some of the principal offices of state. The Tories had had a long run, starting in 1951, and seeing him at close quarters, I sensed that he was weary. Perhaps, deep down, he did not want the job.

He soldiered on for a year at the Foreign Office without doing anything spectacular. When it came to the general election, Alec Douglas-Home ran Labour a lot closer than had seemed likely the year before; but for the unexpected loss of Tory seats in Scotland, he might just have nipped in. So the government which had begun under Churchill in 1951 ended, and we went our separate ways. Butler could have had an earldom, then seen as the prerogative of retiring Prime Ministers, but declined it. Instead, he accepted Harold Wilson's offer of Trinity College, Cambridge. On one of my weekends with Rab – who had won an exhibition to Pembroke many years earlier – I had gone with him for tea with Lord Adrian who was then Master of Trinity. We had gone on to evensong in King's College Chapel. It left me with the impression that Wilson had done the thoughtful thing and that Rab had entered the right harbour. I should have known better. The college was less than enchanted to have foisted on it by a Labour Prime Minister the first non-Trinity man for 250 years. So Rab and Mollie faced a challenge and it took them some time to bring about a change in mood.

To understand Rab's complex mind one only has to read the last book he wrote, *The Art of Memory*, where he expresses more of his feelings than he did in *The Art of the Possible*. Like Anthony Eden, who not long before he died wrote an enchanting book about his early life called *Another World*, Rab seemed reluctant to reveal too much of himself before his final days. I read quite often what Rab wrote in *The Art of Memory* about his first cousin Charles Sorley and the Great War poets. Sorley was killed in 1915 at the age of twenty. His poems, Rab contended, depicted what Sorley's housemaster at Marlborough had called 'an extraordinary thrust of life'. Born in 1902, Rab would have been just too young to serve in that war, and in any case his damaged right arm would have ruled him out, but like many of his generation, he never lost his sense of awe for what those a little older than him had endured on the Western Front. He singles out a poem Wilfred Owen wrote called 'Spring Offensive', which is worth quoting at length, for Rab declares he found it 'almost more than I can bear'.

> Halted against the shade of a last hill,
> They fed, and lying easy, were at ease
> And, finding comfortable chests and knees,
> Carelessly slept. But many there stood still
> To face the stark blank sky beyond the ridge,
> Knowing their feet had come to the end of the world.

Marvelling they stood, and watched the long grass swirled
By the May breeze, murmurous with wasp and midge,
For though the summer oozed into their veins
Like an injected drug for their bodies' pains,
Sharp on their soul hung the imminent line of grass,
Fearfully flashed the sky's mysterious glass.

There is something haunting about those lines. They certainly haunted Rab.

Noel Coward

FOR PART OF HIS life Noel Coward, actor, producer, composer, writer and prolific dramatist, owned a beautiful timbered house in the village of Aldington in east Kent. It had a barn converted into a painter's studio, a view across the Romney Marsh and a glimpse of the English Channel. So when after the war my wife and I bought a house nearby and I was elected the local Member of Parliament, we became acquainted and sometimes met at Cannon Street station on Friday evenings. In those days the best evening train to Kent left at 5 p.m. Driven by steam, it reached Ashford in an hour (about ten minutes faster than today), and it was usually crowded, even in First Class. MPs were entitled to first class travel between London and their constituencies and Coward would not have contemplated travelling any other class, so we both had an interest in securing comfortable seats. 'As soon as you pass the barrier,' Coward once advised me, 'take the first First Class compartment you see. Almost everyone hurries along the platform and passes it.' It was a bit of insight into travel psychology for which I have often felt grateful. 'Ah, the Member!' he would greet me with faintly salacious humour if we met at Cannon Street. His handshake left just the faintest whiff of musk in the palm of one's right hand.

Taking small interest in the theatre, I had seen virtually nothing of his work on the London stage before 1931, though it had included *I'll Leave it to You*, *The Vortex*, *This Year of Grace*, *Hay Fever* and the evergreen *Private Lives*. I arrived to work in London a year after the first appearance of that enduring comedy, which Coward had written in the space of a few days with Gertrude Lawrence in mind. But soon after it opened in the autumn of 1931 I saw his *Cavalcade* at Drury Lane. It made a deep impression on me. At the age of eighteen, I thought it stunning theatre. Opening with a troopship bound for the Boer War – 'We're soldiers of the Queen, my lad. We've been, my lad, we've been . . .' it went on to present a portrait of the first quarter of England's twentieth century, incorporating the Great War and closing with a nightclub scene from the early 1920s. The curtain came down on the leading couple drinking a toast: 'Let's drink to England . . . this country of ours which we love so much'. In one of its superbly presented scenes, the spotlight fell on a young honeymooning couple on the deck of a ship talking softly of their future. It ended in darkness with the spotlight focused on the ship's name, RMS *Titanic*. At the *Morning Post*, where I was working as a young reporter, there arrived an invitation from the enterprising publicity manager of Charles B. Cochran, producer of *Cavalcade*. Would a reporter care to spend an evening at Drury Lane and join those who rode slowly across the stage on the Number 11 bus which featured in a crowd scene in Trafalgar Square on Armistice Night? I was chosen by the news editor to undertake this duty. The experience of going behind the scenes at Drury Lane, watching the moving stage, then playing a minuscule part in the production established Noel Coward in my mind as a genius.

Part of *Cavalcade*'s impact was that it came at an extremely low point in our national life. Wall Street had crashed two years earlier; the Great Depression was upon us. Unemployment in England was high and rising. In the summer of 1931, the Labour government in a sea of troubles had jumped overboard and was succeeded at the insistence of King George V by a rapidly assembled National Government under Ramsay MacDonald. It was the right moment to launch a patriotic play. As the *Annual Register* for 1931 put it later, 'the piece owed what was undoubtedly its strong appeal less to any intrinsic dramatic merits than to its effectiveness as an eloquent appeal for national pride and patriotism at a critical period in the life of the nation.' One of Coward's attributes was his sense of timing. His early plays had sometimes been controversial but they were well suited to the taste of the time. *Cavalcade* moreover demonstrated Coward's strong underlying patriotism, which was later seen in his wartime film script *In Which We Serve* and the poem he wrote in tribute to Bomber Command, 'Lie in the Dark and Listen . . .'. Not everyone, however, saw *Cavalcade* in that light at the time. Coward's detractors thought it out of place for the author of light comedies and *The Vortex*, a play partly about drug-taking, to attempt anything so ambitious. One apocryphal story had

Diana Cooper saying to Coward, 'I saw your *Cavalcade*, Noel, and I laughed and I laughed.' To which Coward responded, 'I saw you playing the Virgin in *The Miracle* and I laughed and I laughed.' But most people saw it as a moving portrait of England and wondered why it did not enjoy a longer run.

Coward's hidden strengths were formed by the disappointments he suffered at different times in his life. The stage is a fickle companion. Coward's fortune was made and unmade more than once. He suffered sharp setbacks in his early days, one of them being *Sirocco* (1927) which starred Ivor Novello and flopped. They never worked together again. He suffered another bout of failure and disparagement in the post-war years. Between 1946 and 1964 six musicals and two plays fell short of his expectations. But he had learned how to live with setbacks without losing the inspiration for something fresh that would succeed.

There was nothing monotonous about Coward's career. He had been born into a family of amateur musicians where his early talents were strongly encouraged, but he was almost wholly self-taught as a composer. The best of his tunes are strongly wedded to his words. 'Extraordinary how potent cheap music is,' he once observed. His tunes caught on. I can remember as a boy whistling one of the earliest and slightest, his *Room with a View*, and I think I included it in my choices on *Desert Island Discs*. A journalist once asked him for what he would be remembered after his death. 'Charm,' said Coward. Counting on this, I paid a call on him one evening in Aldington and invited him to open a Tory jamboree in my constituency. Over strong cocktails and canapés laced with garlic, he cheerfully agreed. On the appointed day I was called to other duties but my wife reported that the charm had worked wonders. He had fulfilled his duties down to the last autograph and had contrived to look as if he was enjoying himself. A mutual friend in the village, A. S. Frere, then chairman of the publishers Heinemann, occasionally threw an evening party where we engaged in what was then a popular pastime, the Game. The Game involved a certain amount of amateur acting. I admired the fashion in which Coward managed to look as much of an amateur as the rest of us.

In 1948, after a disastrous revival in New York of *Tonight At 8.30*, Coward visited Jamaica, loved it, built a house by the sea in the north of the island, and that was where eventually he died. The house, he told me in the 1970s, had cost him £250 and he had recently refused £32,000 for it. His fortunes revived in 1951 with a cabaret spot at London's Café de Paris in which he sang his own songs. A month at Las Vegas doing the same thing brought him $35,000 a week. But our system of taxation was unkind to such earnings in those years and this led him to settle abroad, first in Bermuda and then Switzerland.

It was in Switzerland that I bade farewell to him. In 1971 my wife and I were taking a short summer holiday in Les Avants, a modest winter resort above Lake Geneva across the valley from Caux. There Coward had established his Swiss home in a chalet which years earlier my father had rented for a time. The coincidence encouraged us one evening to pay him a visit. The Master was in bed on the top floor of the chalet, having recently returned from an exhausting ten days in London and New York. At that time his routine was to spend February to April in Jamaica, then do a short season of theatre in New York and London, and then go on to the Swiss Alps. 'May is the best month for Switzerland.'

That evening we found him propped up on pillows, smoking cigarettes, with a clear eye and a bronchial cough. I asked him what he had seen in the theatre. There was a pause and he summoned Cole Lesley, who had come to work for him in 1936 and subsequently wrote *The Life of Noel Coward* four years before his own death in 1980. Well, said Coward to Lesley in his husky voice, what had they seen? There was another pause. Eventually he hit on an Ingrid Bergman play in London. In New York there had been *Follies*. 'We have a bit of money in that,' Coward said in tones of gratification, explaining that most of the shows into which he put money sank.

We discussed his Swiss dwelling, which was next to Joan Sutherland's. After deciding on Switzerland, he made enquiries in Geneva but nothing under £50,000 was on offer. Then his lawyer's son had spotted in the *Daily Telegraph* an advertisement for the chalet in Les Avants going for a mere £11,000. He had added a studio, as he had done at Aldington. 'Ah, painting!' His residence in New York paid for itself because he rented it to friends and so he was content with his lot. There was a big girls' school in Les Avants which occupied what in my father's day had been the town's main hotel. He and Joan Sutherland had visited it for prizegiving. 'Rows of girls who yodel, but they respect my privacy.' So did all the Swiss, he added. Their taxation policy was more lenient than our own.

We talked of Evelyn Laye, whom I had come to know during the war because her husband Frank Lawton had been an officer in my battalion of the King's Royal Rifle Corps. Coward spoke with feeling about the debt he felt he owed her. She had been due to star in *Bitter Sweet*, with its famous refrain 'I'll see you again . . .' when it opened in London in 1929, but she had lately been through a painful divorce from Sonny

Hale, who had gone off with Jessie Matthews when all three were playing in the same Cochran review. The judge had said some hard things about Hale's behaviour which had been prominently reported. In the light of so much dismal publicity Evelyn did not want to face London theatregoers, so Peggy Wood from America had taken the lead. Evelyn Laye took the lead in the New York production, which came later.

Coward had been in New York to see her performance on the opening night in 1930. 'The audience rose to her,' he told me. 'And I knew my fortune – one of them – was made.' There was more to 'Boo' Laye than that, we agreed; more than once she had paid for a chorus girl's indiscretion. I had come to recognize her sterling character during Frank Lawton's last days, when I occasionally popped in during the evening to drink a glass of champagne with him while Evelyn, resolutely putting the traditions of her profession first, bustled off to play in the theatre. Coward himself upheld the stage's tradition of loyalty to old hands who have fallen on hard times; there was more than one of them living in Aldington at his expense.

In October 1972, I went to a revival of Coward's *Private Lives* at the Queen's Theatre in which Maggie Smith was playing, and saw *Cowardy Custard*, a musical medley also running to full houses at the Mermaid Theatre. I sent Coward some account of my evenings at the two theatres. 'Now I seem to have another hit in New York, called *Oh Coward*,' he said in his reply. 'I once had four plays running at once, in the twenties, but never three smash hits at the same time. Now it's happening in my sere and yellow . . . all very satisfactory and highly enjoyable . . . My love to Aldington'. Six months later he was dead, blessed with success at the close of a mercurial life.

In the week Coward died Rebecca West wrote a warm and perceptive piece about him in the *Sunday Telegraph*. Of his homosexuality she observed, 'There was impeccable dignity in his sexual life which was reticent but untainted by pretence.' They were different days from these, and it is pointless to make comparisons. His talent to amuse, some will say, was light in weight, even brittle. Yet it has endured longer than the work of some more serious playwrights. There will long linger on the sunny side of memory some of his comic songs: 'Mad Dogs and Englishmen', 'The Stately Homes of England', 'Don't Let's Be Beastly to the Germans' and 'Don't Put Your Daughter on the Stage, Mrs Worthington'. For many of us he brightened up the drab times which came after the two world wars. He knew the sorry side of human life and in one or two of his plays he touched on it. But it was not in his nature to dwell on it, and that perhaps was because he saw so clearly so many aspects of the human comedy.

Thirty years after Noel Coward's death, while travelling in Jamaica, I visited his last home and resting place, Firefly, with its commanding view of the island's north coast and the Atlantic beyond. Well cared for by a trust, it remains much as Coward left it. There is a pot of Bovril standing in the kitchen cupboard, his clothes hang in his bedroom wardrobe and the walls are decorated with painting done by him or his friends. In a living room downstairs, the music room, most of the space is taken up by two grand pianos, on which stand photographs of friends: Gertrude Lawrence, Joan Sutherland, Gladys Cooper, Richard Burton. On the music stand of one piano the folio is open at 'A Room With a View,' Coward's song which was first heard in a Charles Cochran review of 1928. There are loose pieces of music in almost every room of the house. In his bedroom a large bookcase holds all his favourite reading. The window, through which he could see from his bed, affords a view along the coastline as far as San Antonio, which is miles away. Coward was buried in Firefly's garden where a simple inscription on a marble slab reads:

Sir Noel Coward. B. 16 Dec 1899, Died 26 March 1973.

There is nothing extravagant about the place. On the contrary, there is a monastic simplicity about this slightly untidy villa with its white walls and plain furniture. Climbing the mountain to this place at the summit, the visitor passes Blue Harbour, Coward's first residence in Jamaica. Plainly he sought a place at the very top and that is where he ended his life. 'Sometimes,' I felt moved to write in a newspaper column after my visit, 'the place where a man chooses to die will tell you more about him than you could ever discover in his lifetime . . .'

Diana, Princess of Wales

THERE HAVE BEEN SO many portraits of the late Diana, Princess of Wales, not to mention one or two self-portraits, that one hesitates before putting pen to paper. Her admirers and detractors, most of them holding entrenched views about her, are not seeking further enlightenment. So what is there to add? Well, there are some, particularly those associated with charities she helped, who find it difficult to assess her in the light of all that has been written and said about her, to distinguish between the good and the not so good in her. Furthermore, as a journalist who was fairly close to different phases of Diana's life, I am struck by the extent to which so many commentators focus on the personalities involved, overlooking the part played by newspapers and television and the public mood that they engendered. Between the abdication of Prince Charles's great-uncle King Edward VIII in 1936 and Diana's betrothal early in 1981 there had been a huge social shift in this country. There had been changes in public attitudes towards the members of the royal family and even greater changes in the attitude of the national press.

As Tim Clayton and Phil Craig observed in their book *Diana, Story of a Princess*, 'In the early 1980s the British tabloid press was changing character. Its new face had sharper fangs and a more derisive smirk.' It was principally in the hands of Rupert Murdoch, then an avowed republican and an iconoclast, and Robert Maxwell, whose *Daily Mirror* competed strenuously with Murdoch's *Sun* in the search for sensation. Their editors knew what was required of them.

Persuading readers to recognize their potential, to believe that no one was their superior, was a technique which I associate with Lord Beaverbrook's pre-war *Daily Express*. He was shrewd enough to perceive the social changes wrought by the First World War and to spot how a popular newspaper might exploit them. The colonel's lady and Judy O'Grady were no longer just sisters under their skins; they were lookalikes. So, in the fashion of Shaw's *Pygmalion*, take a shop girl, give her the full treatment, an expensive hat and place her among the grandees in the Royal Enclosure at Ascot and who could tell the difference? With suitable pics it made a grand story. It levelled things up. Like Rupert Murdoch, Max Beaverbrook was what used to be called a colonial, with limited respect for the English aristocracy and its ways.

After the Second World War the trend accelerated. Deference fell out of fashion, which in many ways was for the better: for too long ability had been suppressed because of it. Most of the old social divisions broke down. Public figures came to be judged less by their eminence than by whether they could be addressed by their first names on the golf course. In my earliest days as a Conservative MP in the 1950s, my agent told me to discard the dinner jacket at evening functions with the Young Conservatives. It didn't look matey to dress up. In the late 1960s, when many YCs had acquired evening clothes, my agent advised me to always wear a dinner jacket. It didn't look matey to dress down.

So at the time of the royal wedding in 1981 we were a more equal society than we had been. Extremes of wealth persisted but social barriers were melting fast, except, many would say, at the court of Queen Elizabeth II, which understandably was much slower to change its ways. Why 'understandably'? Because monarchy, in my view, must adapt cautiously to modern ways. In nations moving as fast as we did in the last century, there needs to be a balance struck between change and continuity. So this wedding took place against a social background different from that of earlier royal occasions.

I often noticed that neither Charles nor Diana possessed anything like the self-confidence that we associate with the highly born. When it comes to marriage, the heir to the throne is not his own master and Charles found it difficult to decide until the last moment whether he was doing the right thing. Both his parents were concerned and communicated their anxieties to him. At thirty-three he had established a lifestyle to which he was attached. He appeared to have strong opinions of his own, which he sometimes expressed in public, but he was also prey to acute self-doubts which perhaps had their origins in his unhappy school days. He was not as close to his father the Duke of Edinburgh as he had been to his uncle Lord Mountbatten, who had been murdered by the IRA in August

1979. His mother was not, as some allege, neglectful, but she was unavoidably engrossed in the nation's affairs. He counted a great deal on the support of his grandmother Queen Elizabeth the Queen Mother.

Diana, much younger and unsophisticated – which was one of her attractions to Charles – had failed her O levels twice. Her life up to that point could hardly be described as sheltered, but she was totally unready for the circle she was about to join and for the expectations so many held for a future queen. Diana has been accused of making too much of losing her mother through divorce in the late 1960s, but in truth the loss ran deep with her. So, without a shadow of doubt, did the existence of Camilla Parker Bowles. It is easy to say that in modern times a girl should be able to look lightly upon her husband's past *amours*, but Diana happened to be someone who found it impossible to take such things lightly. The relations between Charles and Camilla nagged her from the start of the marriage and increasingly frayed the knot.

On this not altogether propitious background shone the fierce light of the news media. To be fair, they were catering for what they supposed to be limitless public interest in a long-awaited royal romance. A young beauty who was also the future Queen was fair game. For photographers Diana became the pot of gold at the end of the rainbow. They could not get enough of her. At first it was exciting for Diana, but it soon became exacting. Two high walls enclosed her, an overexcited and insatiable news media and the formidable group of men and women who served the Queen. Seeking to take her role seriously, Diana lost touch with many of her old friends who might have jollied her along. Her future husband was perforce away much of the time on his duties.

Nobody took much account of this until one day late in 1981 when newspaper and television editors were summoned to Buckingham Palace by Michael Shea, the Queen's press secretary, and asked to cool it. Later we moved next door for drinks with the Queen and the Duke of Edinburgh. I was in a small group with the Queen when she observed quietly of a recent incident with photographers, 'It's hard on a girl if she can't go to the local sweet shop without being cornered by photographers.' The then editor of the *News of the World* said rather plaintively, 'Why couldn't she send a footman for the sweets?' 'I think,' said the Queen, 'that is the most pompous remark I ever heard in my life.'

The gathering had little effect: the tabloids were not taking orders from what they regarded as the stuffy old guard at the Palace. They had contacts with some of the royal servants, who kept them erratically supplied with nuggets of gossip, and the photographers worried more about being left behind on a front-page scoop than any reproaches Palace officials could muster. It requires experience, patience and steady nerves to deal with the pack when they are in full cry. As they saw it, their photographs kept Diana in the public eye; without them, nobody would know who she was. She *did* have an eye for the photo opportunity and later she exploited it to the full, but in her early days constant pursuit by photographers – and behind the pack the hidden lens – unnerved her, accentuating the feeling that she was isolated and unprotected. It served the marriage ill.

Diana's phobia about the long lens and consequent loss of privacy extended to her children. When William was young, one or two of us were invited to lunch at Kensington Palace by Diana and Charles to discuss her fears. How would it be, she asked, if while out with his nanny in the park he was taken short and photographed relieving himself behind a tree? That struck us as a bit far-fetched, but not long after William was photographed having a pee behind a tree by one of the paparazzi, and the picture appeared in a German magazine. Not all Diana's anxieties could be written off as neuroses.

The pressures grew. Newspapers and magazines, anxious to feed the public appetite for news and pictures, went to extraordinary lengths to meet demand. The television series *Dallas* attracted enormous audiences, but the Charles and Diana show outshone any soap opera. It is easy to rationalize this, to say it is the price of celebrity, of being a royal, of being a famous good-looking young couple. They're brought up to it, aren't they? It is harder to measure just what the cumulative effect was on a never wholly stable relationship which much of the public saw as a marriage made in heaven. Furthermore, sections of the competitive press were alert to any flicker of doubt, to any hint of unhappiness, of bulimia, of a 'scene'. A thousand ears were cocked for murmurs of discontent and a certain amount did leak from the palaces. This was a relationship under constant surveillance. Diana did behave badly. Her affair with James Hewitt which began in 1986, newspapers are entitled to argue, was more damaging to the marriage than any tale they cooked up. By 1991, the tenth anniversary of their wedding, it was clear that the marriage was under stress, though divorce seemed out of the question. Diana formed other relationships, one or two of them perfectly dotty.

Her next fall from grace was to contribute tape recordings which formed the substance of Andrew Morton's book *Diana: Her True Story*, which the *Sunday Times* serialized in mid-1992. It was a best-seller. For most it fulfilled Diana's aim, which was to appear as the injured wife, but for some it represented a betrayal of the royal family. To just a few, after Diana's denial that she had had anything to do with it, it established her as a liar. There followed charge and counter-charge. There were the 'Squidgy' tapes and the 'Camillagate' tapes, telephone conversations picked up by radio hams which caught both Diana and James Gilbey and Charles and Camilla Parker Bowles in compromising exchanges and which got into the hands of the tabloid newspapers.

At the end of November 1992 fire broke out at Windsor Castle, putting the cap on the Queen's *annus horribilis* as she later called it in her Christmas broadcast. Meanwhile Diana made a series of successful visits overseas. In terms of public relations, she was in the ascendant. There was a minor setback when the *Daily Mirror* published pictures of Diana in a gym wearing a leotard. Furious at this invasion of her privacy, she filed suit against them. The case, mercifully, was settled out of court. Having made her bow to the world, Diana unexpectedly declared at the close of 1993 that she was leaving the public stage, although she continued to court the press.

I attended Jonathan Dimbleby's launch of his documentary and book about the Prince of Wales in June 1994. It was planned by Charles's supporters as a counter-attack but what caught public attention was his admission of adultery with Camilla Parker Bowles. I thought the whole exercise a thumping mistake from his point of view, and so did my editor Max Hastings. One might have expected it to be the last word, but no; Diana was approached by Martin Bashir, who offered her the opportunity to put her case on the BBC's *Panorama* programme. Most of the advice she received warned her against it but she went ahead. The deadline for my thousand words about it coincided with the end of the broadcast, so there was not much time to reflect on what had been said. Nor was time needed for reflection. I thought the interview embodied all the sadness and bitterness which characterizes a broken marriage dragged into the open and would do injury to the monarchy. I was in a minority. The broadcast augmented Diana's host of admirers.

The divorce was agreed in 1996. There was a welcome lull in the storm and Diana's life took a new turn. Discouraged from becoming an unofficial roving ambassador, she sought to address herself to certain issues in the world which were being neglected. One of these was landmines. There were millions of them scattered round the world, lurking wherever there had been conflict. A few charitable organizations were engaged in locating and lifting them, but it was discouraging as well as dangerous work because more mines were constantly being laid in the wars bedevilling Africa. The manufacturers of these mines represented a huge vested interest, which reduced the chances of securing an international ban. Furthermore defence forces in Britain, America and much of Europe saw the mines, properly laid and charted, as legitimate means of defence. For my part, having familiarized myself with the subject since the early 1990s, I had learned the importance of not appearing to deny our own forces a weapon they considered useful.

By January 1997, after discussions with the British Red Cross, Diana had settled on a visit to Angola, a country infested with mines after a long and bloody civil war, some of which I had witnessed. The *Daily Telegraph* thought I should join the party, which included most of the 'royal pack'. Just before we left, I was called to Kensington Palace to provide Diana with my small input on the subject; before flying to

Angola, she did her homework thoroughly. When we reached the wretched capital Luanda there was a sudden change of plan. This, Diana made clear, must be a working visit; the VIPs lining up to meet and entertain her would have to take second place. Supported by our admirable ambassador Roger Hart, she adhered to this throughout our days in Angola.

The journalists, accustomed to covering royal visits in daintier places than Angola, were dismayed by their surroundings. Luanda appeared to have lost its heart and all self-respect. Garbage accumulated on the street corners, the hot weather rendering the stink unendurable. Diana, looking her best in informal tropical gear, seemed thoroughly on top of the job. She delivered a short and sensible speech at the airport, then quickly addressed herself to Red Cross business. They ran a prosthetic centre in Luanda which manufactured artificial limbs, fitted them to amputees and provided the necessary training and therapy. We spent some time there, Diana entering into every detail of the operation and talking with some of the victims. But she had set her heart on going further afield. She wanted to visit Huambo and Cuito, where there had been a siege and brutal fighting during the civil war and which were still infested with mines.

On the day before it was reluctantly agreed to allow Diana to visit these hellholes, there was a lunch in London. Two journalists on the *Daily Telegraph* and *The Times* entertained Lord Howe, a junior minister. During the meal, he spoke critically of Diana's visit to Angola and talked of political interference. After the previous earthquakes, any subsequent tremors set newspaper telephones ringing. Diana's visit to Angola had created a modest stir. If it was causing offence to the Tory government, that doubled its news value. The

Telegraph telephoned advising me that every line of copy I cared to send from Angola would be welcome.

We had flown to Huambo and were standing in a disconsolate group near a minefield. Diana approached me. 'A disturbing night,' I said to her softly. 'Idiot minister,' she replied succinctly. Shortly afterwards, the doyen of our press pack approached me, indicating that it was customary to share any crumbs that fell from the royal table. Had Diana said anything interesting? I visualized the consequences of putting her remark into circulation. 'They had a disturbed evening,' I replied cautiously. Half a dozen young men from the Halo Trust group then greeted her cheerfully and with them she explored a minefield that was being cleared.

The Angola trip was a success, and thanks to the 'idiot minister' attracted more public attention than it might otherwise have done. I ended a long summing-up by writing: 'She has this yearning so many of our younger people have today to take a hand in the world's woes, to tie up wounds, to cherish the afflicted. If the mother of our future King . . . feels drawn in that direction, no matter what form it takes, we should stop carping and doubting. We should be glad.'

Good to her word, Diana intimated her intention to pursue the issue. In the midsummer of 1997 I took the chair for her and helped draft her speech at a conference on landmines under the auspices of the Mines Advisory Group held at the Royal Geographical Society in London. She told me she thought we should make another visit overseas later that summer. With the cooperation of Norwegian People's Aid and Landmine Survivors Network from Washington, a three-day visit was arranged in August. We flew to Sarajevo in a private jet borrowed from George Soros where much of our time was spent visiting victims of landmines. None of them were quite clear who she was, but they all had long and harrowing stories to tell. Diana allowed at least half an hour for every interview, listened intently to each word, flinched at none of the horror stories they told her and then, quite often without saying a word, conveyed across the language barrier a depth of feeling which plainly brought them comfort. We sat alone with a young widow whose husband had been killed by a mine while fishing. With no interpreter present very little could be said. What passed between them is beyond reckoning. When we parted, the widow seemed restored to life. All this in the middle of a fling with Dodi Fayed.

She was an easy travel companion and between the rather grim interviews found time for small jokes. 'Have a gin and tonic!' she would exclaim and then as my eyes lit up would produce from behind her back a bottle of water. Sitting in the back of a car with her, I often scribbled away at copy, pleading like the photographers, 'I have my job to do, ma'am.' Every encounter we had left her with something to think about, so she was often content to remain silent. She made my filing to London painless by allowing me to use her satellite telephone. We finished our tour by looking round the ruins of Sarajevo. It had suffered cruelly during the Bosnian war, with mortar bombs falling constantly on the city, and much of its open space had been given over to the burial of the dead. Diana saw a woman tending her son's grave in one of the huge cemeteries there, walked down to her and embraced her. It seemed the most natural thing to do. There were no cameras in sight. Before we left, our Bosnian hosts asked Diana over lunch if she would consider a visit to Stockholm where they would be discussing an international ban on landmines. I thought it might be politically sensitive and said so. 'You can write my speech,' she said. We agreed to go. Before that month of August ended, she had been killed in a motor accident.

We all have our memories of that day. The BBC called me at home in Kent in the early hours of Sunday morning. There had been a car accident in Paris. Dodi Fayed was dead. Diana was injured but OK. They were sending a car. We were five minutes away from Television Centre at White City when the BBC called my driver. 'Does Lord Deedes know that Diana is dead?' After the BBC, I spent the rest of the day with the *Daily Telegraph* in Canary Wharf, writing all the words they wanted.

It was not until Diana's funeral in Westminster Abbey, on which more words were required, that I fully grasped the extent of the wounds inflicted in the turmoil of that marriage. In one sense Diana had died victorious. The public had come to see her not simply as a wronged wife but as an injured angel. Her sins were not only forgiven her, to many they were endearing. They made her seem human, so much easier to relate to than the woman who occupied the throne and always put duty first. The sinners were to be found in the royal circle, where she had had such a hard time, who now seemed reluctant to lead national mourning for her. The tabloids had a coup de main reserved for them. Why were flags not at half mast? Where was the mourning such a loss called for? Why was the royal family so reluctant to show that it cared?

There was no way of explaining that there were still some people, the royals among them, who preferred to do their mourning undemonstratively behind closed curtains. Spurred by the tabloid newspapers, many decided they wanted the royal family to demonstrate its sorrow publicly. An admirable service, arranged at extremely short notice in Westminster

Abbey, was not enough. There had to be something akin to an act of penance. Those who had failed to appreciate Diana's shining qualities should feel ashamed and be eating humble pie. Lord Spencer, who delivered the address, was loudly applauded for implying as much. While listening to Spencer in the Abbey, my mind crept towards an expression sometimes used by my former boss at the *Daily Telegraph*, Lord Hartwell, about articles and speeches of which he did not altogether approve. 'Bit over the top, I thought,' he would say.

At the root of Diana's unquiet from the start of this marriage lay the friendship of her husband with Camilla Parker Bowles. Most people will blame the Prince of Wales for that; others will declare that her obsession was unreasonable, childish even. Goodness knows, Queen Alexandra put up with far worse from King Edward VII, but that was a different age. I think Diana, largely through inexperience, also found the royal entourage oppressive. It is a pretty rarefied atmosphere and different from anything she had known in her life before, but it was not the main cause of her troubles.

Contrary to public belief, the Queen did her utmost to ease Diana's way. Come to think of it, was the Queen ever likely to make married life more difficult for her eldest son and heir? She did what she could to preserve the marriage. The Queen was understanding of Diana's difficulties and for Diana to imply otherwise, as she sometimes did with loose talk about 'them', was mischievous.

I have always thought it unlucky that Diana's outstanding gifts for sharing grief and for bringing peace of mind to the disadvantaged somehow got lost in palace corridors and the tumult of that marriage. Given more opportunity to display that side, things might just have turned out differently.

Paradoxically, it was not until after her marriage had hit the shoals and wild impulses had driven Diana into inexplicable follies that her gifts began to shine forth. Shortly before her death she had set sail on a fresh course. Who can tell where that voyage might have borne her?

Anthony Eden

THERE IS MORE THAN one way of viewing Anthony Eden's career. Seen in purely political terms, it ended with a misjudgement over Suez, a breakdown in health and a tragic departure from 10 Downing Street: in short, failure. Seen as a whole, his life offers a different impression. In many respects it was a model life given to the service of his country. He came of a landowning family in the north of England which took such duties seriously. Still at Eton when the First World War began, Eden joined the King's Royal Rifle Corps in February 1915. One brother had been interned in Germany on the outbreak of war, his elder brother John was killed. His younger brother Nicholas, a midshipman of only sixteen, was also killed – at the Battle of Jutland in 1916. Eden became adjutant of his battalion, was awarded the MC, and in the last year of the war, at twenty years of age, was made brigade-major, the youngest in the British army.

When the Second World War began in 1939 many of those who had been born at the turn of the century found themselves in uniform again. I encountered Anthony Eden in his old KRRC uniform one evening at a very sodden camp in Hampshire where the recently doubled Territorial Army had gathered for a fortnight's training. Eden had been out of office since resigning as Foreign Secretary in 1938. He was visiting officers of his old regiment, which was allied to my own, and looked perfectly at home with them. He was still only forty-two, no older than my own commanding officer, second-in-command or adjutant. What could be more natural, I remember thinking, than to prepare to serve again with his old regiment?

When war came, however, he was recalled to office, and for the next eighteen years was at full stretch. If we take his starting point in politics as 1923, when he was adopted as Conservative candidate for Warwick and Leamington, his political stint spanned thirty-four years, more than half of them in ministerial office.

He was not a successful Prime Minister, it will always be said, because the call came too late in life. Winston Churchill hung on for too long. That is true, but I think it also questionable whether Eden was ever temperamentally suited to the job. As a junior minister in the Home Office throughout his tenure of No. 10, I formed the impression that he fussed over his ministers too much. He was too sensitive to criticism and too impatient with it. He lacked the broad shoulders which every occupant of No. 10 needs to have.

In those days ministers discussed government business over

telephones made secure by scramblers which took a little time to warm up. 'He will never wait,' one of his Cabinet colleagues once observed to me, 'so you miss the first part of what he says, then have to ask him to repeat it and this irritates him.' But Eden's life at No. 10 occupied a relatively small space in a long career of public service. He was an outstanding public servant, and that is how I choose to judge him.

His detractors like to recall a critical article which Donald Maclachlan, then deputy editor of the *Daily Telegraph*, wrote for that newspaper some months before Suez. It was headed 'Waiting for the Smack of Firm Government' and described how Eden would bring one clenched hand noiselessly into the palm of the other and declare that it symbolized his style of government. That was one view of him. Winston Churchill, much closer to him that Maclachlan ever was, offered a different viewpoint in *The Gathering Storm*. He wrote of Eden's resignation from Neville Chamberlain's government in 1938.

> Late in the night of February 20 a telephone message reached me as I sat in my old room at Chartwell that Eden had resigned. I must confess that my heart sank, and for a while the dark waters of despair overwhelmed me . . . From midnight till dawn I lay in my bed consumed by emotions of sorrow and fear. There seemed one strong young figure standing up against long, dismal, drawling tides of drift and surrender, of wrong measurements and feeble impulses. My conduct of affairs would have been different from his in various ways; but he seemed to me at this moment to embody the life-hope of the British nation, the grand old British race that had done so much for men, and had yet some more to give. Now he was gone. I watched the daylight creep in through the

> windows, and saw before me in mental gaze the vision of Death.

Those of Eden's generation who survived the First World War returned with some advantages. They had crammed so much of life's experience into a year or so and had been compelled to mature quickly. Universities found them unexpectedly good material. Eden resumed his education at Christ Church, Oxford and took first class honours in Persian and Arabic. He abandoned a plan to enter the diplomatic service and chose a quicker route into public service by securing a safe parliamentary seat. While a back-bencher in the House of Commons, he became parliamentary private secretary to Sir Austen Chamberlain, who was Foreign Secretary between 1924 and 1929. It was an unpaid post but it planted Eden firmly on the ladder of promotion. His first experience of office came, oddly, from the former Labour leader Ramsay MacDonald, when MacDonald was persuaded by King George V to put together a coalition government in 1931.

For a couple of months, until the general election that October, Eden as parliamentary under-secretary at the Foreign Office had to answer for his department in the House of Commons because the Marquess of Reading was in the Lords. After the election he continued at the Foreign Office under Sir John Simon, who was not everyone's ideal Foreign Secretary. I encountered Simon a year or so later when I was political correspondent for the *Morning Post*. He came one afternoon to address a gathering of political correspondents, who then numbered no more than a score. '*Gentlemen*,' he began, laying stress on the word, 'and so I address you because I have every desire to be on good terms with you.' With a boss like that,

Anthony Eden could hardly fail to make a good impression. Simon was a wonderfully good lawyer, but unsuited to diplomacy.

Eden first caught the public eye in 1933 when he was appointed Lord Privy Seal – a post like that of Chancellor of the Duchy of Lancaster which is reserved for ministers with special responsibilities. Work at the Foreign Office was mounting: in Europe Hitler and Mussolini ruled unpredictably and disarmament had become a major international issue. Eden's travels included a visit to Moscow for unprofitable talks with Joseph Stalin, the first meeting with a Russian leader by any British minister since the revolution of 1917. Eden was impressed by Stalin. 'Though I know the man to be without mercy, I respected the quality of his mind and even felt a little sympathy which I have never been able entirely to analyse.' Stalin was mainly exercised by the German threat and doubts about Great Britain's willingness to resist.

The Lord Privy Seal was young, good-looking, smartly dressed and wore at an angle a silk-brimmed black homburg hat that was named after him. Some old hands in the parliamentary Conservative party had reservations about him and saw him as a lightweight, but they were prone to take that view of all young promise. My earliest judgement of Eden was unfavourable, because as a war correspondent in Abyssinia during the second half of 1935, I had become cynical about what seemed to be the generally supine attitude towards Mussolini. I had seen oil for Italy passing through Suez as sanctions failed to bring him to book and I had learned with astonishment of the Hoare–Laval plan to award him some of his spoils in Abyssinia. The plan cost Hoare his job as Foreign Secretary, but Eden joined the rest of the Cabinet in supporting such a compromise. When Baldwin summoned him at the end of 1935 and made him Sir Samuel Hoare's successor, my feelings toward Eden were distinctly lukewarm.

But he was still under forty and alongside some of the shabby parliamentary figures who served in the coalition appeared to some a shining beacon of hope. With hindsight, we know now that the Spanish Civil War which broke out in July 1936 was a portent, that Hitler's aims were unacceptable and that Mussolini was a villain. But in my judgement it is unreasonable to expect those in charge of our affairs in those years to have foreseen all this. Even if they had, I have always doubted they could have forestalled it. Churchill's warnings were realistic but related mainly to the military balance between Germany and ourselves.

As one who as a political reporter followed step by step our path down the road to war in 1939, I have become more understanding of the challenge posed by our democracy. Events such as the Fulham by-election of October 1935, the peace ballot and the general election of the same year made it plain that the British public was in no mood to confront the dictators. We were only seventeen years away from the close of the First World War; many still mourned the loss of husbands, fathers, sons. The mood was overwhelmingly for peace, and the Prime Minister Neville Chamberlain did not differ in principle from his Foreign Secretary on the desirability of reaching an accommodation with the dictators. They differed only over method, timing and emphasis.

Eden guarded his territory at the Foreign Office jealously. He was sensitive, a shade too sensitive, to any hint of intrusion. In the early 1950s my wife and I were invited by Conservative Central Office to pay a visit to Austria and talk to farmers. In the middle of our tour Anthony Eden, then Churchill's Foreign Secretary, arrived in Austria to stay with a friend. He was much put out to learn that a Conservative Member of Parliament was chatting up Austrian farmers without the knowledge of his department. He may have had a point; as a courtesy the Foreign Office should doubtless have been informed of my insignificant mission. But there were other instances of this touchiness, and when Neville Chamberlain began to take initiatives of his own in the field of foreign relations, sometimes without informing his Foreign Secretary, it was bound to strain relationships.

An early quarrel with Chamberlain arose over the invitation sent by Hermann Goering to Lord Halifax to some sporting event in Germany. Chamberlain saw this as a means of establishing better relations with Hitler and so did Eden – until it emerged that Halifax would meet Hitler not in Berlin but at Berchtesgaden, which to Eden looked too obliging to the Führer. So Eden, suffering from influenza, protested to Chamberlain, who advised him to 'go back to bed and take an aspirin'. What finally terminated their relations was Chamberlain's desire to give *de jure* recognition to Italy's conquest of Abyssinia. Eden thought that such a concession should be matched by undertakings from Mussolini to pull out of the Spanish Civil War. He also suspected that Chamberlain was orchestrating secret diplomacy in Rome.

In February 1938 Eden resigned, so when Munich became a dirty word, like Churchill he escaped responsibility. Might things have turned out differently had Eden remained at the Foreign Office? I doubt it. Chamberlain would have persisted in his view that given the right handling Hitler could be appeased. Eden, who was under considerable strain at the time, would have broken with him later that year. As things turned out, he was granted a short break from the toils of office before war began.

Eden's war opened unpropitiously. Chamberlain offered him the Dominions Office, without a seat in the Cabinet. In peacetime he might have declined, but after September 1939 refusing posts ceased to be an option. When Chamberlain fell and Churchill took over, Eden was moved to the more important post of War Secretary, but remained out of the War Cabinet. Not until the end of 1940, when Halifax was dispatched from the Foreign Office to the embassy in Washington did Eden recover the post he most desired – Foreign Secretary with a place in the War Cabinet.

There followed the four most strenuous years of his life, which I have always felt sure contributed to his poor health later in life. Being Foreign Secretary was a more exacting occupation in those days than it is now. Air travel was far less comfortable. There were banquets which the Foreign Secretary was expected to attend and address, and as I heard him complain more than once, they came heavy on a tired digestion. As other people's diaries and memoirs make all too clear, Churchill was an exacting master to serve. He got the best out of himself by working through to the small hours, starting the day's work in bed whenever possible and taking a substantial nap after lunch. It worked well for him, less well for those close to him whom he would summon at unearthly hours and who were not in a position to take naps after lunch.

I became faintly familiar with Churchill's routine because for some months I worked as parliamentary under-secretary to his son-in-law Duncan Sandys when he succeeded Harold Macmillan as Minister of Housing and Local Government in

1954. Duncan had learned a lot from his father-in-law. He knew that the best method of persuading civil servants to accept unpalatable propositions, or to resist unpalatable propositions from them, was to keep a discussion going through most of the night. Monday nights were reserved for this exercise. I endured it only for a year and a bit, until Eden, after succeeding Churchill, compassionately sent me to the Home Office. During the war, Eden, carrying infinitely heavier burdens, experienced four years of strenuous days and nights. When at the end of 1942 he became Leader of the House of Commons as well as Foreign Secretary, the burden became well nigh unendurable.

Being outside journalism and politics throughout the war, my only insight into Eden's relations with Churchill rests on what others have written. There is no doubt that Churchill saw him as his successor and so informed the King's private secretary before undertaking one of his voyages across the Atlantic. According to Lord Blake's account of Eden's life in the *Dictionary of National Biography*, Churchill offered him the Middle East Command in 1940 and in 1942 invited him to be Viceroy of India. Both invitations were sensibly declined. Men who leave the House of Commons for such appointments rarely resume their parliamentary careers anywhere near the point at which they left off. Eden's was a pivotal role in the war. He made his share of mistakes but then so did Churchill; victory in war goes to those who make the fewest mistakes. When it was ended Churchill told him, 'Throughout you have been my mainstay,' but physically and emotionally Eden was at the end of his tether. Taken seriously ill with a duodenal ulcer in June, he played no part in the general election of 1945. That same month his elder son Simon was killed in action in

Burma. In 1946 he and his wife separated. His first memorable contribution to post-war politics came at the Conservative party conference of 1946 when he made a speech in praise of a 'property-owning democracy'. 'What a terrible idea!' exclaimed one Labour MP wittily. 'Property-owning democracy.' But the concept became an important part of the Conservative party agenda and, unlike so many political aspirations, it has largely come to pass.

Back on the *Daily Telegraph*'s editorial staff, and by 1947 a prospective parliamentary candidate, I had picked up the threads of politics again sufficiently to perceive that Churchill was not going to take early retirement. The party accepted that Eden was the heir apparent but his succession seemed no closer. Ignoring whispers about his age, Churchill donned what looked like a cross between a bowler and a topper, mounted a horse and was declared to have joined a fox hunt. Labour's majority melted away in the 1950 general election, which was hardly surprising as the years immediately after the war were unforgivingly difficult, and made yet harder by some of Labour's policies, notably the programme of nationalization. For their own reasons Labour ministers were also slow to lift some wartime controls, and after the general election, which reduced Labour's parliamentary majority to seventeen, the Conservatives made increasing play over the issue of unnecessary controls. Labour's senior figures were tired and increasingly harassed by Tories fired by the prospect of returning to office. Aneurin Bevan flounced out of office; Attlee was taken ill. In the general election of October 1951 Churchill got back in with a small majority and Anthony Eden became Foreign Secretary for the third time.

It immediately struck me as a back-bencher that Eden

stood out in the new government as a minister who could be counted upon to master the House of Commons, even on a difficult night. Churchill naturally wanted round him some of the men who had served him well in the war, even if not all of them were practised parliamentary speakers. In those days this was a serious business, particularly for ministers speaking from the dispatch box. I admired the way Eden would sit through most of a difficult debate, retire at about 8 p.m. for dinner at the Chief Whip's table in the Commons dining room, taken with a pint of champagne in a tankard, return to the front bench about 9 p.m., hear the opposition's final speech of the debate and then produce a convincing performance. He still had his critics on the Conservative benches, who I think saw him more as a talented actor than as a statesman. The fact remains that all his performances in the House of Commons were professional, which is more than could be said for those of some of Churchill's wartime cronies.

No denying, Churchill's House of Commons performances in the early months of his return to office were also impressive. At question time he was often witty; in debate on the world scene he was majestic. Bur just about the time when the question of Churchill's succession might have arisen, Eden became seriously ill again. His private life had been restored; he had married Clarissa, daughter of a Spencer-Churchill, the Prime Minister's niece and a loyal guardian of his interests. But early in 1953 he was required to undergo a gall bladder operation which went wrong. A leading practitioner of such surgery once explained to me in painful detail exactly what had happened and why the remedy, for which Eden had to travel to Boston, had to be undertaken. Suffice it, he was out of political action until the autumn of 1953. In June of that year Churchill suffered a stroke. In a fashion unimaginable today, this was kept out of the public eye. The parliamentary session was due to end in a month and the House would not then reconvene until October. The press lords were loyal. The intelligent Christopher Soames, Churchill's son-in-law and parliamentary private secretary, made a good fist of Winston's signature on routine correspondence. The crack was papered over. In the world of half a century ago, it was just possible to control a situation which today's news media would render uncontrollable.

Eden put up with it. Churchill miraculously recovered sufficiently to take over the reins again; he was still at 10 Downing Street in October 1954 when he decided on a government reshuffle. These days this is carried out mainly on the telephone, but because Churchill observed the old courtesies I was unexpectedly summoned to meet him in the Cabinet Room at No. 10 one Saturday afternoon in October and invited to join his administration as a junior minister. Six months later he entertained Queen Elizabeth and the Duke of Edinburgh to dinner at Downing Street and departed the political scene. After the longest wait in modern history, Anthony Eden kissed the Queen's hand as her new Prime Minister.

New Prime Ministers are expected to display a certain amount of buoyancy on arriving at No. 10 and Eden mustered enough of this to impress electors during the general election he called for May 1955. He made good use of the television and his 'property-owning democracy' theme was well received. The government's slender majority of seventeen was raised to a more confident sixty seats. But events turned against him. There were strikes by dock workers and London busmen. Attlee retired and his replacement Hugh Gaitskell gave Labour a sharper edge. Eden did not give the impression of a man who, having waited so long in the wings, was eager to get things done. Government continued much as before, with Macmillan at the Treasury instead of Butler and Selwyn Lloyd at the Foreign Office in place of Macmillan.

The Russian leaders Khrushchev and Bulganin came to London with unfortunate consequences. They paid a brief visit to the Home Office, where by some mischance the Home Secretary and his two parliamentary under-secretaries were not informed of their arrival, and the doorkeepers at the Home Office entrance, which was then in Whitehall opposite the Cenotaph, shunted them into a small waiting room reserved for inconvenient visitors and left them to cool their heels. Meanwhile they were being booed by a small crowd outside. 'Quite right too,' remarked a policeman standing inside the Home Office, as the Home Secretary Gwilym Lloyd George and his two minions, Lord Mancroft and myself, arrived breathlessly and late to greet the Russian leaders. Mancroft thought the policeman's observation droll, and passed it on to a reporter from the *London Evening News* who had appeared. Eden was very angry indeed. Mancroft was summoned for a wigging. 'Put a silk handkerchief in the seat of your pants' – a precaution some of us had learned to take at school before a caning – I said unsympathetically, 'but on no account resign.' It seemed to me that his enforced departure after such an episode would make us all including the Prime Minister look remarkably silly. Mancroft survived.

There is no question in my mind that by the time Eden reached No. 10 his best years were past. His earlier illness and the operations required to put it right had done his nervous system no good at all and he needed prescribed drugs to cope with the demands being made on him. There was muted criticism of him in the party and the press, but it was manageable until just over a year after his arrival at Downing Street, when Nasser nationalized the Suez Canal.

That event and all that it led to has been so thoroughly picked over by so many authors, including the ministers principally involved at the time, that there is no value in rehashing it all again here. Eden was attacked by some for launching the Suez operation and by others for halting it. His cardinal mistake obviously was to ignore or misjudge the likely consequences of his actions in the United States of America. President Eisenhower made no secret of his anger with Britain and her ministers for going to war without the consent of the United Nations. At Westminster the Commons worked itself into the ugliest mood I can ever remember experiencing there. Both the Prime Minister and his Foreign Secretary Selwyn Lloyd were assailed from the Labour benches, which was not very earnestly countered from their own. I have always doubted whether Selwyn Lloyd ever fully recovered his nerve after the battering he received.

On 5 October 1956, before ordering British troops into the Suez Canal Zone, Eden had collapsed with a high fever resulting from his damaged bile duct. He took a short rest and recovered but needed strong medication. On Armistice Sunday he appeared at the Home Office for the Remembrance Day ceremony at the Cenotaph, looking unexpectedly smart and refreshed. Gwilym Lloyd George and I received him. 'He looked OK to me,' I said to Gwilym, who strongly disagreed and expressed alarm at what he saw as the Prime Minister's real condition. His misgivings were soundly based. On doctor's advice Eden flew to Jamaica on 21 November to recuperate, leaving Butler in charge. He returned in mid-December to a demoralized party, and on medical advice resigned on 9 January 1957.

Relieved of the strains of office, Eden's health recovered and he lived for another twenty years. Not long before he died he put his hand to a short and moving memoir of his youth, upbringing and experiences on the Western Front entitled *Another World 1897–1917*, which some of us thought the best thing he had ever written. I know that the letters of appreciation he received from friends gladdened his final days. Inevitably, his name will be forever linked to the Suez debacle and so primarily to political failure. I prefer to see him in another light. Eden came of a family that in both world wars made the supreme sacrifice of its sons. In that tradition, he too spent the best of himself in the nation's service.

Edmund Hillary

EDMUND HILLARY'S CONQUEST OF Everest in May 1953 stirred emotions that ran deep. News of it first reached the crowds lingering outside Buckingham Palace late in the evening before the Queen's Coronation in Westminster Abbey. Though *The Times* had bought exclusive rights to the story, reported for them by Jan Morris then under the name of James Morris, in those days it was thought appropriate to share such news so on coronation day newspaper bills were proclaiming, 'All this – and Everest too!'

Here surely was a sign that talk of a new Elizabethan age was not altogether vain. We had gone through lean years since the end of the Second World War; this achievement was an echo of earlier and ampler times.

The giant range of mountains of which Mount Everest is

part lies between Tibet and Nepal and has no physical links with the British Empire. Yet here was an achievement by a British expedition to awaken memories of 'deeds that won the empire'. My own mind on Coronation morning, I remember, was concentrated mainly on fitting myself into a borrowed suit of court dress and taking my seat in Westminster Abbey at an extremely early hour. Hillary's feat occupied little of my thinking. But in many minds on that day his name rang as the names of Gordon of Khartoum, Cecil Rhodes and Field Marshal Roberts had once rung.

Hillary himself indulged no such thoughts. He had supposed that his feat would be of interest to the mountaineering world to which he belonged, but not to many outside it, and was astonished by the reception he received first in India and then in London. He also underwent the minor but preoccupying worries that often accompany great triumphs. Before the party was halfway back to Kathmandu, a runner reached them with mail and Hillary was taken aback to learn that the Queen had made him a Knight Commander of the British Empire (KBE). 'I did not regard myself as knightly material,' he wrote later. 'For one thing I was far too impoverished to play the role.' A tiresome difficulty also arose in respect of Tenzing Norgay, the Sherpa who had shared with Hillary the final assault on the summit. It was loudly claimed on Tenzing's behalf that he had reached the summit first. Hillary thought this unimportant but among the Sherpas it mattered tremendously. On reaching the summit, Hillary had taken photographs of Tenzing, but omitted to invite Tenzing to take photographs of him. 'It didn't cross my mind,' he says characteristically. 'I was a bit naive, I suppose. But it wasn't important to me.' After a little talk together it was agreed that in team spirit they had reached the summit together, as indeed they had; but that did not stop it entering local lore that Tenzing was the real conqueror of Everest. In a lighter vein, soon after he arrived in London Hillary was examined by Dr (now Sir) Roger Bannister, the first man to run the four-minute mile and a leading neurologist. After the examination Bannister exclaimed, 'I don't know how you did it.'

'What did he mean by that?' I asked Hillary.

'Well, you know,' said Hillary ruefully, 'we came back to the UK and I was very thin. I'd lost a lot of weight, but I was very fit. Then for several months we went to party after party, and I was more or less living on champagne and smoked salmon, something I had never had before in my life. So I went to Oxford and Dr Bannister. He showed me his racemill and raced away. When I got on, I puffed and panted . . .'

The world will long remember that Hillary and Tenzing Norgay got there first. What the world will increasingly overlook, as climbing Everest becomes more and more of a tourist attraction, are the physical risks they encountered in 1953. Experienced mountaineers had lost their lives attempting that same climb. Better equipment slowly shortened the odds but hazards remained. Neither talking to Hillary nor reading the story of his life, *View from the Summit*, does one get a true measure of this, for Hillary is a master of understatement. But when I met him in Melbourne for an interview marking the fiftieth anniversary of the climb early in 2003, he made one observation that throws light on the risks involved. 'We didn't really know,' said Hillary, 'whether it was humanly possible to reach the summit and survive. But when we did reach the summit and I had my oxygen mask off for a quarter of an hour, then everyone knew that you could reach the summit and survive at 29,000 feet . . . a psychological barrier was broken and that was very important.'

It took them five hours to do the final 1,500 feet. 'I think we left at six thirty and got to the top at eleven thirty in the morning. It was a long way uphill and we moved quite slowly. When we reached the South Summit, there was the long narrow summit ridge. Tenzing and I were roped together . . . we had forty feet of rope between us . . . and when I came to the end of the rope, Tenzing came along and joined me . . . then he would belay himself and I would cross another forty feet . . . so it was quite slow.' At that point Hillary had no idea whether they would be able to reach the summit, and as they moved along the summit ridge they came to a rock step about forty feet high which they knew might be a problem. On its right-hand side was a great slab of ice which was breaking away. 'I wriggled inside and wriggled my way up to the top, and when I reached the top of that step (now called Hillary's Step) I knew then that we were going to get to the top. That was the first time I was absolutely confident.' I asked Hillary how much he was carrying. He thought it was about sixty pounds – over half a hundredweight. His oxygen bottle weighed twenty pounds and his Meade tent another fourteen and a half. Why so strong? Heredity? Bee-keeping? The Hillary family's livelihood came from bee-keeping in New Zealand. 'I worked very hard at bee-keeping which is an energetic activity . . . and then I had climbed New Zealand mountains where people hadn't been before and carried eighty pounds in weight. So I was strong and fit.'

Climbing the highest mountain in the world would leave most men feeling that they had fulfilled their mission in life. For Edmund Hillary it was only the start of what he saw as a duty, to improve life for the Sherpas of Nepal who had contributed so much to this triumph for him and the expedition led by Colonel John Hunt. 'I am sure,' Hillary insists, 'that the real regard I am held in almost everywhere is not by any means because I climbed Mount Everest. What has kept it going is activities with the Sherpa people, the building of schools and hospitals . . . we have given back to these people a reward for what they have done for us.'

'You have paid your debt to the Himalayas,' I suggested.

'I paid my dues. That is why people still know who I am. Otherwise I would be forgotten.'

One doubts this but the Queen recognized Hillary's subsequent achievements by making him a Knight of the Garter (KG) in 1995 mainly in recognition of his selfless work for the Sherpas. During the last ten or fifteen years Hillary and his associates have raised about £250,000 a year for the Sherpas in America, Germany, Australia and the United Kingdom.

When the fiftieth anniversary celebrations took place early in 2003, Hillary chose to go first to Nepal and party with the Sherpas rather than come to London with what remains of the 1953 expedition. 'A very human, unassuming, but obviously a very tough, craggy character,' was how the Duke of Edinburgh described Hillary. So this, you might conclude, is a man with very strong legs and an even stronger character. Oh no, says Hillary lightly, 'I am a very weak person – weak at turning people down.' As the anniversary approached, the world's news media beat a track to his door in New Zealand. His telephone rang frequently in the middle of the night because most of his callers did not reckon with time differences. He took all it in good part, conscious no doubt that the publicity would do no harm to his cherished Sherpa charities.

Hillary's family comes from a rural district of New Zealand a hundred miles north of Auckland. He describes his father's personality as a mixture of moral conservatism and fierce independence. His mother, determined that he should have a good education, secured his entry into Auckland Grammar School. The family's bee-keeping ran at one point to 1,600 hives. When the Second World War broke out in 1939, Hillary wanted to join the air force. His father, anxious to retain his services in the family business, arranged work in a reserved occupation without telling his son, and it was not until 1944 that Hillary was able to break away and join the New Zealand Air Force. He was nearly killed in a motor boat that caught fire in the Pacific, suffered severe burns and spent months in an American hospital in Guadalcanal. However, he eventually returned home, healed and with enough money to follow his heart and spend a winter out of bee-keeping in the mountains. After meeting Harry Ayres, New Zealand's leading mountain guide, he climbed Mount Cook, the country's highest peak, and became a proficient ski-mountaineer.

A meeting with George Lowe, schoolteacher and mountaineer, in 1950 led to Hillary's first encounter with the Himalayas. They sought advice from Dr Noel Odell, who had been on Everest expeditions in 1924, 1933 and 1936 and was the last man to see Mallory and Irvine alive in 1924. Then in 1951, with the experienced Eric Shipton and others, they made a reconnaissance of the south-western flank of Everest, though without high expectations. 'No experienced mountaineer,' Shipton had written, 'can be optimistic about the chances of finding a way up any great Himalayan peak. The vast scale on which these giants are built greatly increases the likelihood of the climber being faced by sheer impossibility – an unclimbable wall, slopes dominated by hanging glaciers, or avalanche-swept couloirs.' Shipton put the odds against finding a route to the summit from the south-west at thirty to one. He had said to Hillary, 'Let's go up and have a look round and decide the route is impossible. Then we will head off and explore all those unkind mountains to the East.' 'Which,' observed Hillary drily, 'is what Shipton would have loved to do.' Yet after climbing 20,000 feet and looking at the mountain from a different angle, they found that a formidable but potential route did exist. 'For the first time,' Hillary told me, 'we could see the South Col, and although it looked difficult, it did not look impossible. I was quite staggered. To me it looked as if a possible route did exist on the south side.' That was the way they went.

Eric Shipton had at first accepted the leadership of the 1953 British Everest expedition, though with misgivings, and invited Hillary and George Lowe to join him. Hillary asked that Harry Ayres be invited to join and that was agreed. There was then an unexpected interval until news came through from London to Hillary in New Zealand that Shipton would be replaced by John Hunt. George Lowe described Shipton as a very complex man; primarily, Lowe thought, he was a philosopher. He liked the idea of loneliness. 'He liked the idea of the wildness of the world and he wanted to be there with as small a number about him as possible.' Hillary accepts this view of Shipton as a fair one. So the Himalayan committee in London also had doubts about him. They called in John Hunt, at first with the idea of making him Shipton's deputy, but this was plainly unworkable. Shipton resigned in distress and Hunt took charge.

Much was then going to depend on how Hunt and Hillary got on together. Hillary at first had strong reservations about working under a senior army officer. 'I had modest prejudices against the services,' Hillary told me, 'but what I liked about him was I don't remember him ever issuing a direct order. It wasn't do this or do that and all the rest of it. We would always discuss what should be done. You would express your view and then you'd come to a combined conclusion. As all the climbers were very independent people, he handled them in the best way possible.'

Hunt for his part foresaw that Hillary might be prickly about military authority, and knew how to respond. They first met at the British Embassy in Kathmandu in March 1953. Hillary describes the encounter:

> Striding across the ambassadorial lawn to meet me was a fit, upright, sandy-haired figure – it must be John Hunt. With outstretched hand and friendly smile, he greeted a somewhat reluctant me with, Hello, Ed, I have been wanting to meet you for a long time! My reservations melted even further when John said he was expecting to call on me for sound advice. Obviously, I decided, John couldn't be all bad. It was clear at least that he knew how to handle potentially difficult members.

John Hunt, I told Hillary, had been in my regiment during the war. In a major exercise staged in East Anglia called Bumper, I had been called on to umpire Hunt's rifle company and then tell him what they had done wrong. 'I didn't feel he was an easy man to criticize.' 'No,' agreed Hillary, 'he wouldn't be; but he was a very nice person. He was a good mountaineer himself and he had a very good understanding of mountains. He was good at choosing people to do certain jobs, which really is the epitome of a leader.'

Everest and its approaches have changed a lot more in recent years than Edmund Hillary. 'It has become rather untidy?' I suggest to him. 'Yes,' he says, 'but ten or twenty years ago people began getting a bit more responsible, and a number of expeditions now carry down off the mountain all the junk they have carried up. So the mountain is being cleaned up.'

'And it's got easier?'

'Oh, nowadays there are thousands of inches of fixed rope, there are fifty aluminium ladders over the crevasses in the ice. And then of course there are the tracks of the guides who lead the climbers, most of whom have paid large sums to be conducted to the summit. It's quite an important business these days. We had none of that.' So much has changed, but man's urge to conquer the almost unconquerable, I suggest to Hillary, remains as strong as ever. 'Oh, I agree. The big mountains, the Poles, the depths of the oceans have been done, but there are some very big challenges to come and you need experienced men to do it. There are a lot of extremely good mountaineers and they do some very difficult peaks. They can move quickly because of their equipment. They can climb harder things because of the equipment and they can take bigger risks because of that. We had short clamp irons, but the modern climber has much bigger clamp irons. On the ice face he can bang them into the ice and he can climb a vertical face using clamp-on irons. Now when you can do that . . .'

Edmund Hillary is now in his mid-eighties and high altitudes are out of bounds to him. 'First of all I was only able to be comfortable at 17,000 feet, then at only 13,000 feet. Then for the last couple of years I was only comfortable at 8,000 feet. I think 4,000 feet is my level now. And none of the physiologists know why.' As altitudes started to create difficulties for him, Hillary shifted his adventurous spirit into other pursuits. He led a tractor team across Antarctica to the South Pole. He travelled by jetboat up the Ganges to its source in the Himalayas. He was for two years New Zealand's High Commissioner in India, where he renewed his friendship with Tenzing, who died in 1986 at the age of seventy-three.

Hillary is wrong in saying that he would be forgotten by now were it not for the work he continues to do for the Sherpas by raising money for schools, hospitals, bridges and airfields in the Everest area. A man who climbed the highest mountain in the world for the first time will never be totally out of mind, even to generations born long afterwards. But he is right in thinking that the universal respect in which he is held springs from the way he has set himself to repay some of the people who made his triumph possible. The Victorians are sometimes mocked today for their buttoned-up approach to life and their imperial bombast; but the best of them had a sense of obligation towards those less fortunate than themselves which is not everywhere apparent today. Hillary does not, as some liked to imagine when Queen Elizabeth was crowned, recall the triumphs of our imperial era, many of them won at the point of the sword, but he does embody some of the Victorian virtues which have been cast aside. Precious few of us could follow him to the mountain tops; we do not possess legs like his. The example he set by meeting his obligations to those who served him well is less out of our reach.

Ramsay MacDonald

RAMSAY MACDONALD'S LAST DAY in the House of Commons occasioned a sad little scene in his room. It was May 1937 and a score of newspaper lobby correspondents had been assembled to bid him farewell. He was at Buckingham Palace, we were told , taking leave of the King and Queen, and would join us shortly. We speculated among ourselves on the likely outcome of this visit. Prime Ministers in those days could anticipate an earldom

After about twenty minutes, MacDonald entered the room with a flat parcel under his arm and peered at us. Would we mind, he asked, shifting our chairs so that he could sit with his back to the window so the light would fall on us. As we all knew, his sight was failing. He looked at us silently and then said quietly, 'Ah, Ernest, I'm pleased to see you here.' This was addressed to Ernest Hunter, political correspondent of the *Daily Herald*, which had been merciless in its attacks on MacDonald for what Labour supporters saw as his betrayal of them. Hunter looked as if he wanted to cry.

MacDonald then picked up his parcel and rather clumsily began to untie the string. Their Majesties, he told us slowly, had been most gracious, but he had assured them that he desired no honour or title; it would be sufficient reward if he could receive from their hands a signed portrait of themselves. It was great theatre and only the cynics among us wondered momentarily how this spontaneous gesture had been achieved with the signed portrait already framed and under glass.

We shook him by the hand and he stumbled off for a sea voyage to South America. He is said to have spoken at some point of Tir-nan-Og, the land of harmony and eternal youth which, according to an ancient Celtic legend he had heard from his grandmother, lay west. Worn out, he died suddenly in November of that year.

Ramsay MacDonald's career interests me for a variety of reasons. He rose from penury to become Labour's first Prime Minister. He was for a while the best-hated man in Britain, yet he won his way to power and directed four administrations. Among some of the old Labour faithful he is still thought of as a traitor to the party for consenting to head the National Government in 1931, which swept the country and left Labour with only fifty-two MPs in the Commons. Oddly, he was the first political leader I supported in a general election. Being friendly at school with the son of his first Attorney General Sir Patrick Hastings, I wore a red rosette during the

1923 election. Even to those who knew him far better than I did and were close to him, MacDonald retained a reclusiveness – some called it aloofness – which perplexed people. It helped him, perhaps, to fend off the angry blows that fell on him.

Some time in the 1980s while golfing in Scotland with the late Lord Aldington, we decided to make a short Ramsay MacDonald pilgrimage, visited the tiny house in Lossiemouth where he had been reared in poverty and saw his grave in Spynie churchyard, Lossiemouth, where he lies next to his wife. I remember thinking then that this was a man who undoubtedly brought some of the obloquy he aroused onto his own head but that the demonization may have been a bit overdone. He deserves better of history than the reputation Labour stalwarts grant him, and because the belief that Ramsay MacDonald betrayed his party is so entwined in Labour lore if anyone is going to try to redress the balance it probably has to be a Tory.

I think it possible there were two Ramsay MacDonalds. The first, up to 1911, was a model of the early-twentieth-century socialist. While at school (with fees of eight pence a month) he studied Euclid, read widely, at fifteen was head of the school and at sixteen was offered the job of a pupil teacher at £7 10s. a year. At eighteen he had a job in Bristol – the only city with a nucleus of socialist activity. Then to London, where he tramped around looking vainly for work and starved. After further vicissitudes and earning just enough, he joined the Fabian Society at the age of twenty, applying for membership in a personal letter to Keir Hardie, then the fledgling Labour party's leader. There followed the years in which his Socialist views developed and took shape. He had the luck to work as secretary to a parliamentary candidate. He earned just enough in journalism to keep going and follow his aspirations. He was a good writer, often more lucid on paper than he was in speech. He was an avowed Socialist but strongly opposed to communism, direct action or extremism, and in 1895 stood as Independent Labour Party candidate in Southampton, where he polled 866 votes.

The following year he met and married Margaret Gladstone, daughter of a distinguished chemist and niece of the scientist Lord Kelvin. She had subscribed to his election fund in Southampton. MacDonald was thirty when they married and went to live at 3 Lincoln's Inn Fields. She too was a tireless socialist fighter but she had the gift of making friends and she lent Ramsay an upper-middle-class background. Their 'At Homes' were the first social gatherings the new party had known. As someone put it, 'A hand was laid upon him that softened the rigidity, mellowed and sweetened the vital strength of this restless seeker after an ideal.' When she died in their country cottage at Cosham from blood poisoning in 1911 at the age of only forty-one, Ramsay's tribute to her included this passage:

> To turn to her in stress and storm was like going into a sheltered haven where waters were at rest, and smiling up into the face of Heaven. Weary and worn, buffeted and discouraged, thinking of giving up the thankless strife and returning to my own house and children and household shrines, I would flee with her to my Buckinghamshire home and my lady would heal and soothe me with her cheery faith and steady conviction, and send me forth to smite and be smitten.

After her death, Ramsay MacDonald became a lonely man.

His social circle contracted, and the reserve which many found an obstacle to getting close to him increased. If she had lived, would Ramsay have expressed himself any differently about the First World War? We cannot tell, but it is an important question because his performance during that war saddled him with a burden he never fully shed.

He began by resigning from the chairmanship of the party on 5 August 1914 because it had rejected his proposal that Labour should oppose the government's demand for a war credit of £100 million. His broad line became that Britain was wrong to have entered the war, but having entered must win it, although this measured position was not always reflected in what he said publicly and wrote. For example, his weekly article for the *Leicester Pioneer*, after the speech of Sir Edward Grey, Foreign Secretary, to the House of Commons on 3 August 1914, contained this passage:

> Never did we arm our people and ask them to give us their lives for a less good cause than this. Destitution and sorrow were invited by Sir Edward Grey to come and be with us as our most intimate guests at our firesides. They will accept his invitation, unfortunately, and in the days that will be clouded with their shadow we shall think and feel, and we shall turn upon the authors of our miseries. At the same time, history will be judging and doing justice, and the speech which received the cheers of the vast majority of the House of Commons on Monday will be weighed against the lives of men who will be sacrificed because of it, and it will be dust and ashes, prejudice and error, and nothing more.

Even more provocative was his piece in the *Labour Leader*

entitled 'Why We Are at War', with the subtitle 'The Responsibility of Sir Edward Grey'. Later, MacDonald wrote a letter to the *Morning Post* pointing out that he had declared specifically that, 'Sir Edward Grey strove to the last to prevent a European war.' This fell on deaf ears.

Read through again ninety years on, and after two world wars which in terms of bloodshed exceeded Ramsay MacDonald's worst fears, his words will appear to some at least to be not totally unreasonable, but that view leaves out of account the public mood of those times. A vast wave of patriotism, service and self-sacrifice swept over Britain in late summer 1914, and some of its consequences were harsh. There were calls to imprison German governesses and their like, to hound anyone with a German name or connection. Any man who declared at that point, as MacDonald did, that 'the Foreign Office is anti-German and the Admiralty was anxious to seize any opportunity of using the Navy in battle practice' was seeking trouble.

Margaret MacDonald had been as strong for socialism as her husband; their minds were in harmony. That might at times have been a mixed blessing. She does not sound the sort of woman who would have tried to tone down her husband's speeches or articles. I think it conceivable, though, that she would have been a degree more sensitive to public feeling than her husband. When she died, it was written of her, 'She had so many friends – so many enlightened women were drawn to her by the beauty of her character, by her concern for humanity, and by the sane yet sympathetic view she took on questions of the day – that her influence seemed to be unbounded.' Is it altogether fanciful to suppose that such a woman might have helped her husband better to comprehend the prevailing mood of the time? What fuelled the flames around MacDonald was that German propagandists made good use of what he said, and for a time his speeches around the country were preceded by riots. He became a natural target for the popular press.

Yet the vilification he brought on himself slowly began to have unexpected consequences. Ramsay MacDonald was not one to whine about 'distortions in the newspapers'. The stoical way he bore press and public opprobrium began to stir feeling in his favour. Perhaps the course of the war and the mounting casualties contributed to this, although in the 'khaki' election' of 1918 it did not stop the 'Leicester traitor' from being thrown out of a seat he had represented for twelve years by a hefty 14,000 votes – and this when Labour polled 2.5 million votes for its 361 candidates, fifty-seven of whom were elected. Nor was he much assisted by sounding equivocal about the Russian revolution. His welcome to the first phase of it under Kerensky & Co. was widely interpreted as support for Lenin & Co. But like him or loathe him, MacDonald had become a national figure.

He was out of Parliament for four years, but speaking and writing, editing the *Socialist Review* and travelling extensively in post-war Europe kept him occupied. Early in 1919 he was busy with the international socialist conference in Berne. He was seen as by far the most articulate representative of a party which was rapidly gaining strength in the country. The year 1920 saw MacDonald persuade the annual conferences of the Independent Labour Party and the Labour party to reject communism. The extremists seceded and the abuse they then hurled at him did something to win back the confidence of the public in him.

In 1921 MacDonald lost a by-election in West Woolwich,

where his opponent hammered on his war record, but a year later he won Aberavon comfortably. The same year the Tory party met at the Carlton Club and, strongly influenced by Stanley Baldwin, decided to break with the coalition under Lloyd George, so precipitating a general election. Labour put over 400 candidates in the field and won 142 seats. The Labour vote had risen in four years from 2.24 million to 4.23 million. As for MacDonald at Aberavon, still the object of a vendetta and largely ignored by the press, he scored a personal triumph, polling 14,315 votes against the Conservative candidate's 11,111.

The Tories won in November 1922, but within a year Baldwin had unexpectedly called another election. During 1923, the Labour party leader J. R. Clynes stood down and MacDonald was elected in his stead. Thus when it came to the election in December 1923, in which Labour won 191 seats and the Liberals 159 (a combination of 350, against 258 Tories), a deal between Asquith's Liberals and MacDonald's socialists seemed likely.

Another coalition between the Tories and Liberals was out of the question; Labour governing with conditional Liberal support looked a better option and also seemed fair. King George V saw advantages in giving Labour experience of government and Baldwin had got to know and trust MacDonald, so the 'Leicester traitor' was ensconced at 10 Downing Street.

It has always seemed to me that much of what went wrong for Labour in the short year they held office could be put down to inexperience. For any government 1924 would have been dreadful. There was a slump in trade; unemployment was rising in our industrial centres; the state of farming was dire. In some respects MacDonald's ministry surprised critics by its moderation. Such dark portraits had been painted that some expected a revolution but MacDonald had already won the battle within his party against the revolutionaries. 'It is easier to create a revolution than to make a Cabinet,' he was to remark later.

Labour being opposed to hereditary peerages, MacDonald appointed no new peers but gave Cabinet rank to three men who were already in the House of Lords, but his biggest mistake was saddling himself with the Foreign Office as well as No. 10. He was immersed in international affairs and he did not want a Foreign Secretary who might disagree with him. Though the resulting strain lasted less than a year, it did his health no good, led to neglect of the home front and, indirectly, to an absurd episode.

MacDonald did not take warmly to Downing Street. When he was there in 1931, someone showed me the two gas meters that existed. For the one which cooked his breakfast, he footed the bill. For the other, which cooked for guests, the state paid. It was that sort of place. MacDonald preferred his home in Hampstead, so it came about that the Prime Minister (and Foreign Secretary) could be seen of an evening strap-hanging on the London Underground. To put this right a wealthy Scottish biscuit manufacturer, Alexander Grant, presented the Prime Minister with a Daimler and 30,000 shares in the firm of McVitie & Price for its upkeep – an offer MacDonald accepted reluctantly. Shortly afterwards Grant appeared as a knight in an honours list – though this was not in return for the Prime Minister's Daimler but the £100,000 with which he had endowed the Scottish National Library. It was embarrassing and a bizarre illustration of how we ran the country then, but not fatal.

What was fatal to MacDonald's first administration was a decision approved by his Attorney General Sir Patrick Hastings, new to the Labour party and to politics, to prosecute the acting editor of the communist *Worker's Weekly*, J. R. Campbell, for alleged incitement to mutiny. Campbell had been decorated for wartime bravery in the army, but in an open letter to HM Forces, the *Weekly* had advised, 'Don't allow yourself to be used to break strikes.' Nothing was better calculated to stir up a fuss in the Labour party. In the ensuing storm, the Attorney General – under pressure from a furious MacDonald – changed his mind and dropped the prosecution. The government was then accused of putting improper pressure on its chief law officer. In a motion of censure, the Liberals turned against MacDonald's Labour government, which went down by 364 votes to 198.

In a note to the King, Lord Standfordham, who had been private secretary to Queen Victoria before becoming private secretary to King George V, wrote, 'I saw Mr Baldwin who, in reply to my question "Do you want to turn the Government out?" said, "Yes, but not on the Campbell issue, but on the Russian Treaties which the country generally condemns."' What troubled many people at that point was indeed not the Campbell case, which was certainly a muddle and left the Prime Minister in a bad light, but Labour's policy towards Communist Russia. The government had reversed an earlier decision not to guarantee a loan to the Soviets. MacDonald, overloaded with his self-imposed duties, forfeited the reputation he might have won for moderation by conveying the impression of a government subservient to extremist influences – the very opposite of what throughout his political life he had striven to achieve. This public anxiety about Labour's attitude to

Communist Russia was to have consequences in the 1924 general election.

On 25 October, the Saturday before polling, newspapers splashed a letter purporting to come from Zinoviev of the Communist International, giving British communists instructions on how to start a revolution. *The Times* headline ran, 'Soviet Plot. Red Propaganda in Britain. Revolution Urged by Zinoviev. Foreign Office Bombshell.' The muddle that followed made matters infinitely worse for Labour. MacDonald was out of London campaigning and thoroughly overtired, having left no proper secretariat at No. 10 to deal with such matters. The Foreign Office sent him a draft statement which he amended and sent back expecting it to come back to him again with proof that the letter was authentic. Instead, the Foreign Office published MacDonald's statement as if the Zinoviev letter had been accepted as genuine. The Tories and the newspapers supporting them made hay.

When I arrived at the *Morning Post* a few years later, I got to know Arthur Moyle, press officer at Conservative Central Office. 'He knows the whole story,' I was told. Well he might have done, because Sir Joseph Ball, Central Office director of publicity at the time, had links to the secret service and was suspected of having a hand in bringing the letter to light. I have never thought the 'Red Letter', as it became known, was a Conservative Central Office plot; it would have been too risky. I accept some of the evidence that has since come to light, and reckon it was a spoof. Whether it was genuine or a spoof, it ditched Ramsay MacDonald, and that was a shame. He was once again damned for dabbling with communism, which he had spent much of his political life urging his party to reject. He would have lost the election without the Red

Letter, but probably not by such a margin. The Tory vote rose from roughly 5.5 million in 1923 to over 8 million a year later. The Labour vote rose as well – at the Liberals' expense – but they won only 151 seats against the Conservatives' 419. After barely a year in office, MacDonald was consigned to five more years as leader of the opposition. What he wrote after his defeat tells us something about him:

> Sometimes one must flee from familiar things and faces and voices, from the daily round and the common task, because one's mind becomes a bit of green grass too much trod upon. It has to be protected and nursed, and it has to be let alone. Then, give me the hill road, the bleating of the sheep, the clouds, the sun and the rain, the graves of dead races, the thatched roofs of living ones, a pipe and a fire when the day is closing, and a clean bed to lie upon until the sun calls in the morning. If friends fail, the hill road never does.

The Conservatives' years in office 1924–9 were not momentous but will be remembered for the General Strike of 1926 and for the prolonged strife in the coalfields after which we never exported coal again. MacDonald, an opponent of direct action, called the General Strike a 'weapon that cannot be wielded for industrial purposes. It is clumsy and ineffectual. It has no goal which, when reached, can be regarded as victory.' These were years, we need to remember, when industrially this country was slipping downhill. That is what lay behind the long war of attrition between owners and workers.

Much of MacDonald's time was taken up with healing the differences within his own party. Our industrial plight widened the gap between Jimmy Maxton's small Independent

Labour Party and the main party MacDonald led. 'We can no longer stand by and see thirty years of devoted work betrayed in making peace with capitalism and compromises with the political philosophy of our capitalist opponents,' declared one ILP manifesto in 1928. MacDonald's line was: 'With the Labour Party in existence and the ILP affiliated to it, the ILP cannot go on as an independent party of Labour laying down political policies of its own, trying to impose political policies of its own, trying to impose a superior allegiance for itself, defying the decisions and the policy of their colleagues in Parliament.' MacDonald sometimes looked a muddler, but he never deviated from his view that Labour's ideals were better achieved by gradualism than by revolution.

On a visit to the United States in 1927 he was taken seriously ill. Arriving there tired, he was infected by a wasting disease rampaging across the Middle West. He recovered in the air of his native Lossiemouth, largely ignoring a warning that at sixty-one even his apparently indestructible physique had limits. The Conservatives remained in office long enough to grant Winston Churchill as Chancellor of the Exchequer his fifth Budget in April 1929. Parliament was dissolved on 10 May, the day MacDonald issued his election address to the electors of Seaham. 'You have to elect a new Government. Is it to be reactionary, or is it to be Labour?' he wrote. Then he set off on a grand tour of the country, making half a dozen speeches a day, keeping the issues of unemployment and peace to the fore. His Scottish tour alone covered a thousand miles. He ended up with a broadcast from the Newcastle station of the BBC on 28 May. Labour won 288 seats, a gain of 126; the Conservatives secured 260 seats, a loss of 140. The Liberals held the balance of power with fifty-eight MPs.

It was about this time that the American economy began to show signs of serious disturbance. By July 1929 industrial production was in decline; in October employment was falling and the stock market started to slide. On 24 October, a day on which thirteen million shares changed hands and the market crashed. My mother wrote to tell me that my father was in serious financial difficulties and I left Harrow a year early. In November Ramsay MacDonald's government announced £42 million worth of public works. 'Too little, too late,' said the Tories and so it seemed. By March 1930, unemployment here was 1.5 million, a rise of 500,000 since Labour had taken office. By August it was two million, having doubled in fourteen months. MacDonald had included Margaret Bondfield in his Cabinet as Minister of Labour, the first woman to hold such rank, and, as I describe elsewhere, Jimmy Thomas was told to find solutions to unemployment, assisted by Oswald Mosley. MacDonald had a few minor triumphs. His chairmanship of the India Round Table conference in 1930, paving the slow road to independence there, was widely admired. He paid a visit to President Hoover in the United States and made progress on naval disarmament. But the economic tide continued to roll in over such achievements as if they were sandcastles.

In his biography of King George V, Kenneth Rose remarks that it is doubtful whether any government could have surmounted the world slump in trade and the financial crisis of 1931, but that MacDonald's response was memorably inept. That is fair comment. Part of the trouble was that to preserve the country from bankruptcy, MacDonald's ministers were called on to take action that ran directly contrary to their strongest political beliefs. That is a hard thing about politics:

events may call upon a man to do something wholly contrary to his political creed. If he does so, his party will accuse him of betrayal; if he does not, then he will be seen as a man who put party before country.

I arrived to work in London at the *Morning Post* in time to hear everyone talking about the 'May report'. In March of that year the government had appointed an independent committee under Sir George (later Lord) May, formerly of Prudential Insurance, to report on how national expenditure could best be reduced. The committee calculated that the government would be £120 million in deficit by the end of 1932, largely due to the soaring cost of unemployment. May proposed a cut in unemployment pay by two shillings to fifteen shillings a week for men and thirteen for women. The dole should not be paid for more than twenty-six weeks in one year and unemployment insurance contributions should be increased. This was not what the members of MacDonald's Labour Cabinet supposed they had been elected to do. Summoned back from their summer holidays, they were dismayed by what was being asked of them and dug their heels in. They were prepared to accept £50 million in cuts but not a further £22 million reduction in unemployment benefits. MacDonald continued to press for economies that would balance the Budget. Meanwhile, the May report was frightening investors and the gold reserves were falling. On 23 August MacDonald reported to the King that he and his colleagues could not agree a way forward. The King saw Stanley Baldwin and Herbert Samuel separately. The National Government began to take shape. Philip Snowden, Chancellor of the Exchequer, Jimmy Thomas, Lord Privy Seal, and Lord Sankey joined MacDonald. Had he succumbed to what they called at the time the 'aristocratic embrace'? Did he want his government to fall? Did he agree to what he thought would be a temporary solution? I think MacDonald did see the National Government as a short-term solution, what was called at the time 'a doctor's mandate', but we shall never know for sure. 'I have changed none of my ideals,' he declared in a broadcast. 'I have a national duty.' Life would never be the same for him again.

The cuts led to threat of a naval mutiny at Invergordon. The pound was devalued, the gold standard abandoned. Montague Norman, Governor of the Bank of England, warned of bankruptcy. In the autumn general election, in which I was too young to vote but able to report, the coalition won with a landslide. Ramsay MacDonald, titular Prime Minister, had the support in the Commons of 473 Tory MPs, thirteen from his own National Labour Party and sixty-eight assorted Liberals. There were just fifty-two MPs from his old party in opposition. Labour's bitterness over what Herbert Morrison called 'betrayal' reached new depths. MacDonald was reported to feel at ease with his new colleagues, which increased Labour fury, and he probably did find his Cabinet of ten – four Labour, four Conservatives and two Liberals – easier to handle than a divided Labour ministry.

Because I did occasional political reporting for the *Morning Post*, I had a fairly close view of MacDonald's four years as Prime Minister 1931–5. It was an untidy Government. Ironically, one of his government's first steps was to impose the tariffs which Baldwin had wanted eight years earlier and which had cost him an election. The Liberal element of the coalition found that hard to swallow, so there was an agreement to differ and the government split into two camps, with John

Simon leading one and Herbert Samuel the other. A believer in personal diplomacy, MacDonald sought in the House of Commons to justify a meeting with Mussolini in Rome, but he was by no means the only Prime Minister vain enough to believe in the power of such face-to-face meetings. Plans for a federal constitution for India took shape. Compared with what was happening in Germany, however, it was all rather small beer.

MacDonald did accept at an early stage that appeasement must be accompanied by some restoration of our sadly depleted armed forces. Through the 1920s and early 1930s, disarmament had been the goal, but in November 1933 MacDonald's government admitted that the policy of cutting arms spending as an example had failed. The first, tentative – and some argue wholly inadequate – steps to put our defences in order were taken. At the *Morning Post*, a true blue Conservative newspaper, the word was that MacDonald's powers were beginning to flag, or, less euphemistically, that he was becoming slowly dottier. He made one or two speeches which encouraged this belief, speaking at one point of his government going 'on and on and on, and up and up and up'. I encountered him at a Londonderry House reception where he was resplendent in white tie and tails but looked somewhat detached. He had worn himself out, but in the early days of the National Government he was seen as an indispensable figure, endowing a mainly Tory administration with the appearance of a broad coalition.

In June 1935 MacDonald resigned the premiership on grounds of ill health but remained in the government as Lord President of the Council. A big crowd at Euston saw his exhausted figure off to Scotland and a piper played, 'Will ye no come back again'. He lost his seat at Seaham in the general election of November 1935. Game to the last, he scrambled back into the Commons in a by-election for Scottish Universities in January 1936 but died the following year.

To most Labour hands, both old and new, Ramsay MacDonald will long be seen as someone who betrayed his party by consenting to lead a predominantly Conservative administration cobbled together in the critical days of 1931. A fairer judgement might be that, at the behest of King George V, he consented to put country before party.

Imelda Marcos

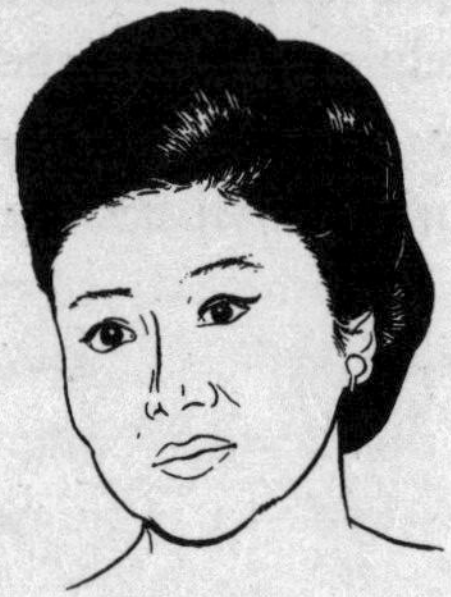

ONE THINKS TWICE BEFORE including a portrait of Imelda Marcos in this small gallery. Widow of Ferdinand Marcos, sixth President of the Philippines, she is famous primarily for colossal extravagance in a very poor country; but she is also part of the history of the twentieth century. How she and her husband, who died in 1989, clambered to power and contrived to stay there for twenty-one years tells us something about the world and its ways. Imelda Marcos is a survivor, and the way in which she survived is an instructive tale. I met her only once, at a small dinner party she gave in the Malancanang Palace in Manila just before the Marcos regime crashed. But I returned later to pick up the threads, to discover more of what had happened and to meet the new President, Corazon Aquino, whose husband, Benigno, a political rival of

Ferdinand and Imelda Marcos, had been shot dead at Manila airport when returning from exile in 1983.

The story opened for me in May 1984 when the minister at Japan's embassy in London invited me to lunch. As editor of the *Daily Telegraph* I had no close association with Japan, so the invitation was unexpected. He began by saying that the Marcos regime in the Philippines, of which I knew virtually nothing, was unlikely to survive much longer and that its collapse might threaten the future of America's two huge facilities there, Clark's air force base and the Subic Bay naval base. That in turn might alter the balance of power in the Pacific. President Gorbachev of the Soviet Union had been speaking of the Pacific as a lake that should be shared. The prospect troubled Japan. Perhaps, my host at lunch suggested, the *Daily Telegraph* might feel inclined to take a look at what was going on in Manila.

Our Far East correspondent Ian Ward, whom I consulted, was based in Singapore, knew the Philippines well and many of its leading characters. He would make such appointments for me as he could and meet me in the Manila Hotel. Before leaving I collected as much literature as I could find about Marcos and his wife, and then flew out via Kuala Lumpur. Ferdinand Marcos had been a brilliant, daring and by some accounts ruthless young man. In the 1950s he had been charged with the murder of Julio Nalundasan, an arch political rival of Ferdinand's father. Marcos was found guilty in the lower courts but was acquitted by the supreme court. Imelda came of an impoverished branch of the well-connected Romualdez family. Beautiful and ambitious, she had come to the attention of the public by winning a beauty contest.

So she was in the public eye towards the end of 1953, just

before she met Marcos. As a congressman with ambitions to become President, he was seeking political entry into Manila's elite, while Imelda was striving to gain social entry into it, so they had something in common. He proposed to her in April 1954. How a dashing congressman won the hand of a beauty queen in eleven days caught the headlines. A month later a thousand guests crowded into the cathedral to see them married. At first, it was an awkward match. Imelda was twenty-five, her husband thirty-seven. Imelda, whose childhood had been spent in poverty, was unprepared for her husband's life style and felt an outcast. Marcos wanted her to be what she was not. Winning a beauty contest had not prepared her to mix with the wealthy and sophisticated, but eventually she mastered the role she was required to play. The first big challenge came at the Nationalist party convention of 1965 where the presidential candidate would be selected. There were 1,347 delegates to be won over and Imelda charmed them all. But having won the vote, they had to find a suitable running mate for Marcos. The man they wanted as Vice President, Farnando Lopez, refused to enter the race, declaring that he was old, and sick and tired of politics. Imelda went to work on him. One of her assets was an ability to cry at will. It won him over. During the campaign itself, Marcos's Liberal opponents raised the old murder charge against him, but in vain.

So in November 1965 the Marcoses entered the Malacanang Palace to rule over fifty-four million Filipinos. Imelda got quickly into her stride with the creation of an extravagant cultural centre. During the years they were in power, it stood as a symbol of her ambition and relentless drive. Such a couple was bound to attract enemies, and in 1970 one of them produced a book, *The Untold Story of*

Imelda Marcos, revealing her poverty-stricken childhood. The Marcoses sought by every means to suppress it – by buying out the rights, by intimidation, by threat of libel. It was an important book because it gave people an inkling of what lay behind Imelda's extravagance: she was banishing the ghost of an impoverished childhood which had for so long haunted her.

Re-elected in 1969, Marcos won the election largely by falsely presenting himself as someone who would stand up to American imperialism. In reality, he secured billions of dollars in international bank loans with US support. By one means or another the money at Imelda's disposal soared. Public funds and private income were inextricably mixed. She was ranked as the tenth richest woman in the world and her spending sprees in New York and London consolidated this reputation. In a country where per capita income was barely $200 a year, her personal wealth was reckoned to be $250 million in 1972, the year Marcos declared martial law the only way (he claimed) to stop insurrection by the Communist party of the Philippines. In effect, he imposed a dictatorship.

Senator Benigno Aquino, an opposition leader who might otherwise have defeated Marcos in the 1973 election, was arrested and cast into jail. There he staged a forty-day hunger strike which severely damaged his heart. Doctors recommended bypass surgery and for this, after much thought, Marcos and his wife agreed he should be permitted to go to the United States. Fully recovered from a triple bypass operation, he resumed his attacks on Marcos and warned him of a gathering storm.

What held the storm off was the support of the United States of America. A new agreement on the bases raised the rent from $500 million to $900 million for five years and

Imelda cruised expensively around the world. She joined world leaders at the inauguration of President Nixon. In London, she spent two hours at No. 10 with Ted Heath. 'Goodness, the woman could talk . . .' he is reported to have said afterwards. She made friends with Castro in Cuba. Her most celebrated conquest, she confirmed at our dinner party, had been Colonel Qaddafi. She spent relentlessly and there is some evidence that the Philippines National Bank received instructions to disburse funds to Imelda from an 'intelligence account'.

Marcos lifted martial law in 1981 and won his last election. 'We love you, sir, we love your adherence to democratic principles . . . and we will not leave you in isolation,' intoned Vice President George Bush. But Marcos was suffering from serious kidney problems and word was getting out. The external debt of the Philippines had risen to $18 billion. Aquino, weary of his exile in the United States, threatened to return home. Imelda took pains to dissuade him, warning him he would be killed. Ignoring her Aquino persisted, and in August 1983 flew into Manila on a China Airlines Boeing 727. Outside the airport building 20,000 people awaited his return. Passengers on the plane were told to remain seated as soldiers entered to fetch the celebrated exile. As they hustled him through a service door, a single shot was fired and killed him.

The country was engulfed in political turmoil. Marcos found it necessary to appear on television to deny that Imelda had had a hand in the killing but America reckoned that the Marcoses were too smart to be implicated. Aquino lay in state in his own home and three million Filipinos attended his subsequent funeral. Imelda went on spending. Ferdinand Marcos got sicker. The country's economy became more desperate. By the spring of 1984, when I reached the Malacanang Palace, the skies were very dark indeed.

Ian Ward's influence in Manila proved invaluable. The Palace, he told me after some telephone calls, had promised a small dinner party, and President Marcos would submit to an interview the following morning. The mood of desperation accounted for our welcome; America was growing restive and difficult, and a newspaper editor from England was a straw to be grasped. Ian and I spent the morning kitting ourselves out for Imelda's dinner party. The start of our evening was unnerving. We were shown into a huge gallery where portraits of earlier Presidents were hanging and spent some time alone there. We were not to know that an elaborate scene was being set next door.

Eventually a lady-in-waiting – known in Manila as a blue lady – joined us. This was Carmen Nakpil, mother of a Filipino beauty queen. Would we like a drink? She rang a bell and ordered whiskies and sodas, but before they arrived, doors were flung open, lights blazed and we were ushered into the presence. I was seated on a sofa beside Imelda, who was dressed in an expensive black creation which became her perfectly. Other guests sat in the shadows. We were outnumbered by the television crew and their acolytes. Most dinner parties begin with light talk over drinks and then progress towards more serious conversation at the dinner table. Imelda Marcos reversed this routine. Television lights beating down on us, she gave me a recital of her woes. It had been a terrible year with drought, floods, financial difficulties, her husband's illness and the killing of Aquino. 'A political disaster,' she pronounced, looking me in the eye.

It was twenty minutes before a servant dared step forward

with my whisky and soda. Imelda's dissertation lasted forty-five minutes. She displayed a mastery of facts and figures that I found impressive without knowing whether they were true or not. It was nine o'clock before we reached a dinner table laden with cutlery and glasses for five courses and four wines. The food was not memorable, the wine was delicious. We were a small company of seven, comprising Imelda, her blue lady, the British Ambassador and his wife, the Deputy Governor (to Mrs Marcos) of Metro Manila, Ian Ward and myself. Our hostess moved swiftly from the national and international scene to the story of her life. She had been one of eleven children, and all of them had played a different musical instrument. Her mother had been a singer; Imelda herself had a remarkably good voice. Her early marriage to Marcos, she told us, had been frugal and Marcos had rebuked her for spending nearly half the housekeeping money on flowers. But this was essential, she told him, for their love must be surrounded by beauty. Part of this tale was invention – Marcos was not a poor man – but their love story was genuine enough. To the very end it survived all vicissitudes. They were kindred souls.

Imelda held forth at length and unselfconsciously about beauty and its spiritual values. None of us were called upon to respond; this was a recital. While the waiters attended to our needs, we sat in silence listening to this figure in a short black frock adorned by a single jewel and a snatch of bright silk at the throat. She spoke of General MacArthur. His marriage, she told us, had not been successful and he had been in love with her aunt. Soon after MacArthur had fulfilled his famous vow to return, Imelda had watched them from an upstairs window in a passionate embrace on the beach. Her aunt had never married, but had died a month after MacArthur. This was the stuff of a great movie such as *From Here to Eternity*, which was popular in the 1950s.

She told us of her encounters with Colonel Qaddafi, whom she had found very macho. 'You seem a reasonable woman,' he had told her, and begged her to embrace the Muslim faith. After giving her a marked copy of the Koran, he had sent her a dozen copies. He had also, she declared, sent her a romantic telegram. When alone with him, she had told him, 'You are a good man, a religious man.' This had kept him at bay. Imelda had recounted all this to Vice President Bush, who had asked the then head of the CIA to debrief her. At the end of a four-hour session, she explained, they had popped the inevitable question: 'Did you sleep with Colonel Qaddafi?' 'What a question to ask a girl!' exclaimed Mrs Marcos to us. The dinner party was like one of those plays during which, in order to enjoy yourself, you have to suspend belief. Some of her tales were intended to convey her philosophy of life. When visiting the Vatican, she encountered a school friend who had failed all her examinations. 'Where do you live now?' Imelda had asked her. 'Here,' said the school friend unexpectedly. She was working on needlework for the Pope and had found total fulfilment. It proved, Imelda sought to assure us, that all human beings had a value.

It was past midnight when we left. The Deputy Governor had fallen asleep. Perhaps he had heard it all before. Ian and I took leave of her back in the drawing room with its banks of flowers and signed portraits of international figures. Imelda showed no trace of fatigue. Her eyes were bright, her complexion fresh, the pile of dark hair on her head still faultlessly arranged. 'I feel indebted to you for an unusual experience,' said the Ambassador to me as we awaited our cars in the Palace forecourt. 'Not one we are likely to repeat, Excellency,' I replied. Back at the Manila Hotel, Ian Ward and I agreed to stay awake another hour in order to note down all we could remember.

Next morning Ward and I returned to the Palace for our interview with Marcos which, like the evening with Imelda, was filmed, but was not half so interesting. Some journalists believe aggressive interviewing produces the best results. In my experience people like Marcos reveal more of themselves if you coax rather than cross-examine them. So I treated him emolliently, some would say obsequiously. 'Let's hope none of my friends see the video of that interview,' I said to Ward as we left. Marcos bestowed on me some of his writings and I later received the video of our conversation as a memento.

Lee Kuan Yew of Singapore warned President Reagan that the end was nigh, and Marcos unwittingly precipitated it at the end of 1985 by telling David Brinkley of American television that he proposed to hold a snap presidential election. Eyes turned to Corazon Aquino, widow of the murdered man. She had sound qualifications – for she had been educated in America and bore her husband's indomitable spirit – but she was reluctant; her husband had declared that whoever came after Marcos would sink within a year. In the end she agreed to enter the election on her own terms and fought a spirited campaign. When the election took place in February 1986 Marcos was declared the winner, but after such palpable fraud that America withdrew its support. Cory Aquino called for a national disobedience campaign to upset the result. Marcos demanded the arrest of his Minister of Defence and Chief of Staff as conspirators. They defected and barricaded themselves in an army base. The very oddly named Cardinal Sin urged people onto the streets and told the nuns of Manila to fast and pray. Thus the widow of Marcos's murdered rival was swept to power. Marcos despairingly sought the guidance of America's Senator Laxalt who was in Manila. 'Cut and cut cleanly . . . the time has come,' said the Senator. A few hours later the Marcoses were flying to exile to Hawaii. They had had a good run for their money.

I went back to Manila a few months later. They had stopped the looting at the Malancanang Palace so I was able to walk through the long corridors of booty, displaying Imelda's vast collection of clothes and shoes, the gift racks of watches and clocks and expensive gadgets for presentation to friends, admirers and acquaintances. The heels of Ferdinand Marcos's shoes, many of them unworn, were slightly built up to make up for the inch or two he stood short of Imelda. There was a small well-stocked underground hospital ready to deal with his various complaints. It struck me that the United States, so dependent on the Philippines and the Marcoses for its hold on the Pacific Ocean, had been careless with the petty cash.

Then in the presence of President Aquino I attended a vast parade outside Manila to mark the first anniversary of the revolution that had swept her to power. She invited me for a talk and I wished her well, while reckoning that her husband had been right – that the corruption of the Marcos era would soon render her burdens insupportable.

Dame Lilo Milchsack

DAME LILO MILCHSACK, WHO founded the Anglo-German conferences at Königswinter in 1950, holds a place in my mind as one of the architects of post-war Europe. Elegant, intelligent and determined, she used her gifts as a leader to heal some of the wounds Britain and Germany had inflicted on one another during the war years and brought them towards a better understanding of each other. I have rarely met a woman who could so readily persuade other people to do her bidding and leave them feeling that they had been favoured.

After a meeting with her in the House of Commons one afternoon in the 1960s, I escorted her to the Members' exit to find a taxi for her next port of call, the German embassy. As we waited, I spotted a chauffeur at the wheel of a Rolls-Royce. He was awaiting an MP whom I knew. 'Look here,' I said. 'This is one of Germany's leading citizens. Will you run her to the German embassy? I'll square things with the boss.' The chauffeur looked at me as if he doubted my sanity, then he glanced at Lilo Milchsack standing beside me, got out of the car and opened a door for her. She had that effect on people.

There are many romantic tales woven around her founding of the Königswinter conferences. My favourite version, which I think is not far off the truth, begins with her marriage to Hans Milchsack, one of the biggest barge-owners on the Rhine. Lilo Duden, as she was before her marriage, had been born in 1905 at Frankfurt, the granddaughter of the compiler of the famous Duden dictionary, and was educated at Frankfurt, Geneva and Amsterdam universities. She came to England in the 1930s to stiffen resistance to Hitler and fell foul of the pro-Nazi Anglo-German Fellowship. Meanwhile Hans was doing some resistance of his own. Hitler had called together wealthy figures in the Ruhr and made an appeal for funds. Lilo Milchsack once took me to see the room in Düsseldorf where this took place. Hans not only refused to give Hitler money but returned home from the gathering in such an overwrought state, it is said, that his wife thought he had drunk too much.

As enemies of the Nazi regime, the Milchsacks had a hazardous war. Towards its end, when Allied bombers were pounding the Ruhr, Lilo and her two daughters slept in an air raid shelter at their home near Düsseldorf, Lilo with a ring containing cyanide on her finger. At the end of the war Hans became mayor of their home town of Wittlaer. Then Lilo suffered a nervous breakdown. As she recovered, Hans offered her any thanksgiving gift she desired. 'I'd like not to have another war,' she is reported to have said, a wish that led to the founding of the Königswinter conferences. What is certain is that for the early years of those gatherings Hans Milchsack paid most of the costs.

It is one thing to conceive an annual gathering of people of influence in Britain and Germany with a view to dispelling misunderstandings, quite another to make it an event to which people are eager to be invited and will, if asked, come year after year. Dame Lilo and her followers imparted that touch to the Königswinter gatherings. Some of her entourage had been open opponents of Hitler throughout the war and had been lucky to escape with their lives. I used to look at some of them, then ask myself whether I would have had the guts to defy Hitler from within Germany and receive a disappointing answer. A familiar figure in the early years of the meetings was Axel von dem Bussche, who had lined his clothes with explosives in a thwarted mission to dispose of Hitler. Several of the Germans, including Christabel and Peter Bielenberg, Hans von Herworth and Marion Donhoff had extraordinary experiences to recount. Königswinter brought home to one that to show strong disapproval of Hitler from within Germany during that war counted for extreme valour.

In the early stages of the Deutsch–Englische Gesellschaft, Lilo Milchsack had some useful British allies as well. One of them was Robert Birley, educational adviser to the military government in the British zone of Germany and later headmaster of Eton. He had helped Lilo and her friends in the Red Cross to deliver relief to the vast number of foreign workers in Germany and had invited her to England. One of the first Germans to visit Britain after the war, she went on a Foreign Office-sponsored visit to Norwich and Cambridge.

There was a marked difference between this country's feelings towards Germany after the First and the Second World Wars. After 1918 there had been calls to hang the Kaiser and to squeeze Germany for reparations until the pips squeaked. Churchill, true to his adage 'in victory magnanimity', had at one point proposed sending food ships to Germany, but his proposal had provoked the newspaper headline 'Hun Food Snivel'. After 1945 the mood was less pugnacious. Hitler was dead; much of Germany had been hammered to bits. Those Nazi leaders who had survived were about to be tried in Nuremburg. The German people were seen by many – though not all – as victims of a tyranny the Allies had managed to crush. The main objective was not to punish Germany but to cautiously revive the country and return her to democracy.

Lilo Milchsack saw the need for an exchange of views about Germany's future in Europe. She told Birley of friends in Germany who would help promote the Anglo-German gatherings she had in mind. However, the kindness she had received during her visit to England also caused her to fear lest this generosity led the British again to fail to understand what her own harsh experience had led her to think was the darker side of the German mind.

Part of her genius lay in devising the right formula for the gatherings and sticking to it. So often deep thinkers turn out to be bad organizers. Lilo was an exception. The invitations were limited to sixty a side. They went to Britons and Germans interested in public affairs – politicians, journalists, diplomats, academics, bankers and industrialists. There was nothing confidential about the proceedings and the broadsheet newspapers usually carried some account of the weekend's work. The usual mix was one third old Königswinter hands, one third frequent attenders and one third newcomers. That played well. We would fly out on a Thursday afternoon just before Easter and attend a convivial dinner party at which German wine flowed freely and brief speeches were made. Friday morning would open with a plenary session at which pre-selected speakers introduced three or occasionally four topics. One of them usually related to Britain's place in Europe or progress in the European Community. Another looked at the state of East–West relations; the Berlin airlift had ended in 1950, the year Königswinter held its first meeting. The third or fourth subject would centre on the issue of the year – environment, demography or the workings of the news media.

The opening speeches and comments on them occupied the first morning. We would enlist before lunch for whichever topic most appealed to us, and spend the first afternoon and much of the following day thrashing it out in a group, assisted if necessary by interpreters. On Sunday morning rapporteurs from each group would report their findings to a plenary session. This would produce a final battery of short speeches from the floor. On Sunday afternoon everyone returned home. It all sounds rather mundane, but it worked a treat and proved that close attention to small detail is the making or breaking of a successful conference.

All this was useful, but in Lilo Milchsack's mind establishing friendships was also important so she insisted that time was left for social events, formal and informal. At an early conference I recall crossing the Rhine one afternoon with Dick Crossman in order to take tea with Konrad Adenauer, Germany's first post-war Chancellor. What we said to each other I forget, but I remember the extremely shallow cups in which our tea got very quickly cold. Sometimes we would cross the Rhine on coaches for an evening reception at the British embassy in Bonn. On the second evening the Mayor of Bonn or the German government might provide hospitality. Sometimes the German political parties offered supper parties to their British opposite numbers. When these entertainments were over the beer houses in Königswinter would be open and those so minded would form groups for idle talk. In the beer house of Robin Day's choice, Germans and British would probably end the evening by singing together *Lili Marlene* or *Ilkley Moor*.

It looked deceptively simple at the time, but putting it together called for imagination. A Königswinter steering committee assembled the main business; Lilo Milchsack's staff in Düsseldorf looked after the detail and her personality bound it together. There were other attractions to this long weekend, such as walking along the Rhine and watching the long processions of barges go by, or climbing the local mountain, the Drachenfels, before breakfast.

The first fourteen conferences were held in the austere setting of Adam Stegerwald-Haus, a Catholic trade union hostel and discussion centre where the old hands were rewarded with bedrooms. The lesser lights were more comfortably housed in the hotels of the small riverside town. In 1964, for the first time, the British acted as hosts – at Oxford. In 1970 we met at Cambridge and in 1974 at Edinburgh, in 1976 and 1978 in Oxford again. Thereafter the pattern became even-numbered years in Germany and odd-numbered years in Britain.

Wherever it took place, the conference attracted an impressive number of British political heavyweights, especially from the Labour side. Glancing through a list of British participants in 1962, I see the names of Tony Wedgwood Benn, Violet

Bonham-Carter, Patrick Gordon Walker, Roy Jenkins, Chris Chataway, Kenneth Younger and John Strachey. That was the year I was appointed rapporteur for a group discussing 'Changes in the Communist world – what are we doing about it?' I cannot imagine anyone but Lilo Milchsack persuading me to take on such a task. Her letter of thanks to me afterwards contained this passage: 'I always have had something of a bad conscience towards those who have to work so hard at Königswinter, as I do realize what a strain it is to report in a very muddled discussion! Every member of your group agreed that you resolved your task marvellously and that your clear-cut résumé was brilliant and enjoyed by everyone.' I reproduce this not out of vanity but simply to illustrate the turn of phrase with which Lilo Milchsack won friends and influenced people.

In pursuing her aim for better understanding between Britain and Germany, she also arranged for brief speaking tours for some of us. I undertook one of these in 1957 and spent a week travelling between Berlin, Hamburg, Essen and Stuttgart. The lectures were delivered in English, the hospitality was generous and the company informative. I did another tour for her in 1965. Travelling through Germany on Lilo Milchsack's behalf, one seemed always to be in the folds of a magic carpet. At the airports there was invariably a welcoming face to greet you. Meals were not ordered, they arrived. I felt ashamed of not being able to put together a sentence in German, but this was considered no impediment to lecturing. My audience, I was assured, would understand every word in English. On one of these tours I spent a night or two under the Milchsacks' roof and was impressed by the absence in their home of any show of wealth. The bathroom, as I remember, could have been modelled on those in slightly impoverished English country houses.

On Sunday afternoons, as the conference at Königswinter broke up, those who wished were flown east for another couple of days in Berlin. I sometimes chose to do this simply because the city was so full of interest for a journalist. The Berlin Wall was up and ugly, but arrangements were made for us to pass through it and visit East Berlin to view conditions there. It has never surprised me that Germany later found the East such a tremendous pill to swallow.

It is open to those constantly mistrustful of the country which started the two great wars of the last century to suspect that those of us who made this pilgrimage to Königswinter were too easily persuaded by this able and attractive woman to think well of Germany; that behind all the careful arrangements lay an element of propaganda. If that were so, I doubt whether she would have succeeded year after year in attracting people like Gladwyn Jebb, Dick Crossman, Barbara Castle, Walter Elliot, Roy Jenkins, Shirley Williams and David Marquand. Furthermore, as some of us knew, Dame Lilo Milchsack's purpose was not to make us love the Germans more but to develop a clearer understanding of their nature. That dark side troubled her; she had, after all, survived it.

The springtime conferences continue, but in Berlin, so she left a legacy, but it is pointless to speculate on what people like her have contributed to history. Let us only say that someone who could persuade Germans and British to enjoy sitting round a table solemnly to discuss the Oder–Neisse line was out of the ordinary. Lilo *was* out of the ordinary.

Field Marshal the Viscount Montgomery of Alamein

I COUNT IT A LUCKY day when Andrew Burnaby Atkins, the only platoon commander in my company to get through the battle for Europe unscathed, dropped me a line in 1947 asking if I would care to dine with him and his boss, Field Marshal the Viscount Montgomery of Alamein. A year earlier Montgomery had succeeded Lord Alanbrooke as Chief of the Imperial General Staff. He chose as his aide-de-camp Burnaby Atkins, who had won an MC and bar in Europe. What could be more normal than that Burnaby Atkins should invite his old company commander to dine with his new boss?

There was rather more to it than that, I later came to surmise. Among Montgomery's characteristics was a strong appetite for personal publicity, and after the war I had rejoined the *Daily Telegraph*. That gave me a touch more value than as simply his ADC's former company commander. We had a congenial dinner together, *à trois*, in the Field Marshal's London flat. Though himself an abstainer, Monty had no objection to other people imbibing. It was the beginning of a long acquaintance.

To most of us who had lately returned to civilian life, Montgomery was a hero. His desert victory against Rommel at the battle of El Alamein in October 1942 had been our first taste of victory in the war. Church bells, which had been restricted to warning of enemy parachute landings, had rung out joyfully. Since then, intelligent mice have nibbled away at the mistakes he made in north Africa, later in Sicily and Italy and in Europe where he commanded XXI Army Group under General Eisenhower. They have criticized his caution, his propensity for quarrelling with America's generals, his tactlessness and his small vanities.

Montgomery *was* idiosyncratic, dogmatic, tactless, quarrelsome. Those failings had dogged his early days in the army. It speaks well for his superiors in the more socially sensitive years between the two wars that they chose to brush aside such failings and, recognizing a winner, continued to promote him. I have always believed that Providence, or whatever you wish to call it, played a big hand in the Second World War. Montgomery was our commander at El Alamein because W.H.E. 'Strafer' Gott of my own regiment was killed on his way to take command of the 8th Army.

During the battle for Europe I never met Montgomery, though I once encountered him. He was standing on the beaches of Normandy in mid-June 1944 when I landed with two thirds of my motor company's vehicles. The other third had drowned in the shallows due to damage done to their waterproofing during loading at London's docks. The dockers had refused to load vehicles for which there was no prescribed rate and my riflemen had done the best they could.

Monty's table talk was brisk, assertive and delivered in the clipped tones of military command, but stimulating.

> Attlee worn out. An awful job. Seen him in the Cabinet room alone – absolutely exhausted, with piles of files both sides of him . . . Future Prime Ministers? Bevin? Sick man, very sick, no future . . . Three good men – Tom Williams, Chuter-Ede and Shinwell. Asked Churchill what he thought. 'Hrrmph . . . I asked those three to join my Cabinet.' Have regard for Shinwell. Likeable chap. War Office done him much good. First thing, went and saw him. 'Delighted to see you here.' Much appreciated. Now would do anything for me. Got him just right. We get on fine.

He was revealing too on wider aspects of the Second World War. 'Alamein. Churchill wanted it in September. "No," I said. "October." We argued. I said then, "If we go in September, I don't say we shall fail, but we shan't get there. If in October, I guarantee success. Which is it to be?" His decision then. He said, "October." That's essential. Politicians bully. You must put decisions squarely to them.'

Having taken part in our narrow failure to win Arnhem bridge in the autumn of 1944, which prolonged the war, I listened to Monty's view of it attentively.

> Failure to win by Christmas. All our troubles hinged on that. Americans did not realize how vital it was we should win. They were not exhausted. We were. Patton [Commander, America's 3rd Army] or me – didn't mind

> which. One of us should have been sent on. Not a single effort. People talk as if there were one armoured division on one road [Guards Armoured Division]. But a million men sweeping on! Then think – Patton in Czechoslovakia, the bridge between east and west. And me in Berlin. None of this trouble [with the Russians] would have arisen. Russians were well back.

After a simple three-course meal served by a sergeant, with water to drink but wine on offer, Turkish cigarettes appeared. He had no objection to smoking. 'I only don't because I don't like it.' A bad period in the war, he told me, was in the late summer of 1944 when our armies were striving to break out of the Normandy beachhead. It was an uncomfortable time, during which we all suffered a steady stream of casualties. Alanbrooke had called up Montgomery from London with a complaint from Eisenhower that America was suffering more than her share of casualties. Were we saving our soldiers at their expense? Montgomery protested that the Americans lost more soldiers because they were less skilful. Churchill had emphasized the need to minimize casualties. He spoke movingly, according to Montgomery, of the losses we had suffered in the First World War. Similar losses this time round, Churchill thought, would threaten our future as a nation.

My wife and I joined Monty at El Alamein night in London in October, anniversary of the battle. He revelled in the echoes of that victory and the lustre it had conferred on the 8th Army. It awoke echoes in me too, for soldiers singing sentimental songs, sometimes on the eve of battle, strikes a deep chord in some of us. He presented me with a bound copy of his personal messages to the 8th Army 'in the hopes that the younger members of the family will gain some inspiration from these messages which were used to inspire the soldiers of the British Empire in days of great peril'.

How strangely those messages read now. This is the start of the message 'to be read out to all Troops' which he produced on 23 October 1942, on the eve of battle:

> 1 When I assumed command of the Eighth Army I said that the mandate was to destroy Rommel and his Army, and that it would be done as soon as we were ready.
>
> 2 We are ready NOW. The battle which is now about to begin will be one of the decisive battles of history. It will be the turning point of the war. The eyes of the whole world will be on us, watching anxiously which way the battle will swing. We can give them their answer at once: 'It will swing our way.'

This epic concluded:

> 5 Therefore let every officer and man enter the battle with a stout heart, and the determination to do his duty as long as he has breath in his body.
> AND LET NO MAN SURRENDER SO LONG AS HE IS UNWOUNDED AND CAN FIGHT.
> Let us all pray that 'the Lord mighty in battle' will give us victory.

Montgomery was not loved by his contemporaries in the British services, being all too prone to argue with them, and was positively detested by America's top brass, but he found a path into the hearts and minds of the soldiers he commanded and planted confidence there. That was one reason for his success.

There was another side to him which I gradually came to know. Like many of his kind, Montgomery had never known a home for any length of time. He married in 1927, but after ten years of happy marriage, much of it overseas, his wife died in Britain of septicaemia after an insect bite. Thereafter he buried himself in the army. In January 1940 a German air raid on Portsmouth destroyed his personal possessions, and after the war ended and he had received the highest honours, his thoughts turned to the home of his dreams.

He found Isington Mill in a small valley below the London–Winchester road at Bentley in Hampshire. There he designed his home much as he had planned his battles, but getting it built was another matter. All construction work in those post-war years was rationed, so his local council felt unable to grant permission. The Field Marshal threatened to plant himself and his collection of caravans in an adjoining meadow. The authorities faced a dilemma. True, a grateful nation had given Marlborough Blenheim Palace, but this was the century of the common man. What if a pacifist raised questions in the House of Commons about preferential treatment for Montgomery? But then again what if the victor of El Alamein was found camping in a field? At the highest level authority yielded.

So the great plan advanced and at one point I was invited to inspect progress. New Zealand, Canada and Australia had chipped in with the timber which was the mill's main distinction. Floors, doors, staircase, cupboards and wardrobes were all composed of unstained Empire woods, and local craftsmen had knitted them together in a wonderful exhibition of English joinery. The design, with one great sweeping room on the ground floor, was not to everyone's taste, but it was *his* design without advice or interference from anyone else. There his innumerable trophies could be properly shown off and his many portraits hung on the walls.

Representing different phases in his career, they were a study in themselves. The earliest, I think, had been painted after El Alamein by an official war artist, a South African. There was James Gunn's study of him in a polo-neck jersey and a more formal portrait in uniform by the same artist. Frank Salisbury's painting had been done after victory in Europe. The latest was by Oswald Birley, painted after he had left Whitehall as Chief of the Imperial General Staff.

He liked one to study these portraits and was delighted if one came to the conclusion that Rommel and Runstedt had left fewer signs of strain on him than his three years in Whitehall among the politicians. I remember feeling most moved when I looked at all this. It was the first settled home of a man of sixty who had led the vagrant life of a soldier and whose treasures were not heirlooms or from salesrooms but the fruits of his own achievement.

Oswald Mosley

MY FIRST ENCOUNTER WITH Oswald Mosley, leader of the British Union of Fascists, was in Aldgate on a Sunday afternoon in October 1936. He had just led 2,500 of his Fascists along Royal Mint Street with the intention of marching through the East End of London. Aware of this, crowds had gathered in the streets to stop him. They were being held back by cordons of mounted and foot police, 3,000 of whom were on duty. At this point Sir Philip Game, Commissioner of the Metropolitan Police, appeared on the scene. Nowadays, one would expect to see the Commissioner in uniform but this was a Sunday in the 1930s so he was in country clothes, which somehow heightened the drama. Reckoning that he was about to confront Mosley and that a reporter's job is to be in the right place at the right time, I manoeuvred myself closer to him.

On a street corner next to the Royal Mint, he summoned Mosley, drew his attention to the crowds blocking all roads to the east and told him that the march must be called off forthwith. It was a bizarre scene which might have been taken from an ancient battlefield. Game in his country tweeds had one or two senior uniformed officers beside him. Mosley in his black uniform stood alone, looking like a defiant chieftain, but he was smart enough to demand of Game if this was to be taken as an order. Yes, said Game. Mosley went off to convey this to his own officers, and his procession turned westward and marched smoothly along the Embankment to Charing Cross where it was dismissed. Mosley was thus able to claim that the BUF was a disciplined and law-abiding force. Even so, the afternoon produced a score of broken heads, considerable damage to paving stones and windows and eighty-four arrests. My account, headed 'Many Arrests in London Riot', made the *Morning Post*'s splash on Monday morning.

This is the Mosley most people visualize when his name crops up today. Mosley in a black shirt, leading a bunch of thugs into east London and revelling in the disorder thus created. Mosley, aping Europe's dictators, Hitler and Mussolini. Mosley the anti-Semite, provoking violence against the Jews of Whitechapel. That was indeed the Mosley I saw most of in the 1930s but, many years later, in the 1970s when I was editing the *Daily Telegraph*, he invited me to lunch with him privately in London. These later encounters led me to wonder why on earth a man blessed with almost all the gifts needed to succeed in politics so perversely chose the course he had.

In the search for clues I think one has to start with the First

World War. Not long before it broke out, the seventeen-year-old Mosley had persuaded his family to let him leave Winchester and train as a regular soldier at Sandhurst, so when war came he was able to get a commission with a good regiment, the 16th Lancers. Bored by inactivity because the cavalry was not in demand, he switched to the Royal Flying Corps and won his pilot's licence. He survived a flying smash, returned to his cavalry regiment, then spent the last two years of the war working in London at the Ministry of Munitions and the Foreign Office. He later described the feelings that went through him when the war ended:

> At the Armistice in 1918 I passed through the festive streets and entered one of London's largest and most fashionable hotels, interested by the sounds of revelry which echoed from it. Smooth, smug people who had never fought or suffered, seemed to the eyes of youth – at that moment age-old with sadness, weariness and bitterness – to be eating, drinking, laughing on the graves of our companions. I stood aside from the delirious throng, silent and alone, ravaged by memory. Driving purpose had begun; there was to be no more war. I dedicated myself to politics, with an instinctive resolution which came later to expressions in my speeches: Through and beyond the failure of men and of parties, we of the war generation are marching on and we shall march on until our end is achieved and our sacrifice atoned.

'Tom' Mosley, as his friends called him, was not the only young man to experience such feelings, to feel bitterness against those who had presided over the slaughter of their friends, and to resolve to do something about it. But he was better placed than most of his contemporaries to practically respond to these instincts. Heir to a Staffordshire baronetcy and estate, good-looking and well-connected, he had made a series of conquests of influential women, through them had met influential politicians and, being well regarded in social and political salons, was soon in demand by Conservative and Liberal whips for Parliament. He was chosen as Conservative candidate for the Harrow division of Middlesex in time to join the election which swiftly followed the armistice. At twenty-two, he became the youngest MP and one with a majority of 10,000. He was the golden boy. A year later, while helping Nancy Astor to win Plymouth, he met Cynthia, second daughter of Lord Curzon, Viceroy of India and Foreign Secretary in Lloyd George's coalition government. By March 1920 they were engaged to marry. So to his own not inconsiderable wealth was added the fortune which Cynthia had inherited from her grandfather Levi Leiter, the Chicago millionaire. They became a gilded and sought after couple, smartest of the smart set.

You may take the view that up to that point it had all been too easy for this young man and that he was spoiled; or that as a man with strong opinions of his own he was bound eventually to rebel against 'the old gang'. At any rate, he fell soon fell out with his Harrow constituency association, which decided not to back him in the 1922 election. He stood as an independent, yet still won with a majority of over 7,000. But after the election at the end of 1923, which Baldwin called and lost on the issue of protection, and in which Mosley's majority fell to 4,600, he began to feel the need of a political home. Burning his boats with the Conservatives by abusing their record – 'drift buoyed up by drivel' – and swiftly wooed by the

Labour party, he was received into their fold with a warm letter from Ramsay MacDonald in March 1924.

It was a time for anyone closely interested in politics to take stock. The Great War had cost us valuable markets, including our coal exports. Our basic industries were in decline and being overtaken. In search of solutions, Mosley read Keynes but formed economic theories of his own and gave expression to them in a pamphlet called 'Revolution by Reason'. Arrogant by nature, he could not abide being constrained by the disciplines which all political parties have to maintain. He had invincible confidence in his own views; everyone else was out of step. He got back into Parliament at the end of 1926, being returned as Labour candidate for Smethwick with a large majority. Two years later he inherited the baronetcy. In 1929, his wife 'Cimmie' was elected Labour MP for Stoke-on-Trent. There was even talk of Tom becoming Foreign Secretary in the new Labour government. Instead he was made Chancellor of the Duchy of Lancaster, a post usually reserved for ministers with special responsibilities. In this case, Mosley's was finding solutions to unemployment under Jimmy Thomas, formerly secretary of the railwayman's union and now Lord Privy Seal. Thomas was a card, a man of limited ability and poor judgement – as he was to prove later by blabbing about a Budget – but also the author of endearing wisecracks. 'Jimmy, you're selling us!' a heckler called out at a railwaymen's meeting. 'I'm trying but I can't find a buyer,' responded Thomas. He was a man unlikely to convince someone like Mosley that the way ahead lay through the usual political and parliamentary channels. Mosley has described the weekly meeting he and Thomas held with the heads of departments involved with the unemployment problem: 'These admirable people listened with patience to the trivial absurdities with which J. H. Thomas sought to mask his complete failure to understand the real subject.'

In their forlorn quest Thomas and Mosley were assisted by George Lansbury at Works and Tom Johnston, Secretary for Scotland, but unemployment – from a smaller workforce than we have now – remained obstinately at just over a million, where it had been for six years. Mosley decided to take an initiative of his own. He produced a radical memorandum early in 1930 which in the short term recommended road building, in the longer term more state intervention and the equivalent of a War Cabinet under the Prime Minister to see it through. Keynes pronounced it an able document. In his own account Mosley claims to have kept Thomas informed about the memorandum but admits that a copy entrusted to John Strachey somehow found its way into the hands of the press. Angered by this, Thomas threatened to resign. The long-suffering MacDonald persuaded him to stay on and sent a rebuke to Mosley. Certain members of the Cabinet, however, were not taken with Mosley's ideas, which led to their rejection in May 1930. Mosley then resigned. Meanwhile the Wall Street crash of 1929, heralding the Great Depression, was upon us and creating despair. Mosley's last hope was that his popular appeal and skill on the platform would persuade the Labour conference of October 1930 to support him. When that endeavour failed he set about forming the New Party, which was launched in March 1931. Mosley later described his mood at this point in these terms: 'I was determined to have a decision between action and inaction, and if the party refused to take action I felt it my obligation to seek other means to secure it.

This was not a young man's impatience, it was a different concept of public life and duty.'

The Western world was in a bad way and so were we. As a newspaper correspondent I travelled the country enough to perceive the plight we were in. I had witnessed and reported the collapse of the cotton industry in Lancashire. I visited all the so-called Distressed Areas, talked to families in South Wales who had never held a job, saw the derelict shipyards of Tyneside, reported the arrival in London of the Jarrow marchers. I am not suggesting that Mosley's remedies would have succeeded, but the state of the country helps to explain his anguished state of mind. Partnership with a clown like Jimmy Thomas under the wobbly hand of Ramsay MacDonald was to prove the last straw. Capitalism everywhere was in low esteem. It was fashionable for progressive minds to visit the Soviet Union, where despite the suffering of the population at the hands of Lenin and Stalin they claimed to have found a better way. In Italy, Mussolini had resorted to direct action. In Germany, Hitler was about to do the same and his action initially met with some grudging approval here while in its early stages. So Mosley's New Party, which was at first conceived entirely in parliamentary terms, rang few alarm bells. It also failed to attract public support. In the autumn election of 1931 he had hoped to win a dozen seats, and against MacDonald's Labour party he might well have done. Against the Conservative, Liberal and Labour coalition backed by a more or less united press, Mosley stood little chance. All his twenty-four candidates were defeated, receiving an average of 1,036 votes apiece. Mosley himself polled 10,543 votes.

Late in 1931 Lord Rothermere, owner of the *Daily Mail*, told Mosley that he was ready to put the Harmsworth press at his disposal if he could produce a disciplined movement from the New Party. Early in 1932, Mosley visited Italy and there the seeds of fascism were sown in his mind. Cimmie was repelled by the idea. Mosley took up fencing again. It had been his favourite sport when as a young man at Sandhurst. He quickly became proficient, and at the age of thirty-five with an injured leg he was runner-up in the British épée championships. It absorbed some but by no means all of his abundant energies. On 1 October 1932, one year after his rout in the general election, the British Union of Fascists was launched.

For a couple of years it floated respectably – sustained by Mosley's powerful oratory and Rothermere's *Daily Mail*, it was strongly influenced by Mussolini's Italy and Mussolini at this point was not without admirers in this country. Then came an abrupt change. I missed the Olympia meeting of June 1934, where the violence made big headlines. Someone at this point suggested to me that Mosley had been advised by Mussolini that a successful revolutionary movement needed to make enemies. For every dozen or so enemies, he would win one or two staunch adherents and thus create the nucleus of an irresistible movement. I have never known if any such message did reach Mosley's ear, but his tactics from that point on suggest that it might well have done. Moderates who had taken Mosley's economic theories seriously and supported the New Party took fright and backed off. One of them was Harold Nicolson, who wrote, 'If Tom would follow my example – retire into private life for a bit and then emerge fortified and purged – he will still be Prime Minister of England. But if he gets entangled with the boys' brigade he will be edged gradually into becoming a revolutionary; and into that waste land I cannot follow him.'

As a resident of Bethnal Green I witnessed a good deal of what followed. Mosley's meetings and marches came to resemble military patrols. They were intended to be provocative and were unquestionably anti-Semitic. Events in Whitechapel, Stepney and Bethnal Green, I wrote in an article for the *Morning Post* in October 1936, 'offered a disturbing glimpse of the bitterness and hatred which six months of active political and racial strife had generated in the East End of London'. Why the East End? Because Mosley, deprived of his middle-class support, had turned to the streets and there raised an issue he knew to be divisive. 'Until now,' I wrote, 'the most important party in the dispute has remained strangely quiescent. To their credit the Jews have suffered humiliation and insult without retaliation.' I sensed that their patience was exhausted and that they would strike back.

As it turned out, it was not the Jews but the communists who struck back, relishing a fight with Mosley's fascists. Perhaps the changes which had come about in Mosley's private life accounted for his more aggressive tactics. Cimmie had died of peritonitis in May 1933, but even before her death Mosley had become close to Diana Guinness, third of the Mitford sisters. In October 1936 Mosley married her privately in Hitler's presence. It is tempting to see hovering over that match the shadow of Unity, the Hitler-obsessed sister, but according to his son Nicholas, Mosley had turned to fascism before he met Diana.

From then on, Mosley and his movement became of less account. With growing awareness that war with Hitler was becoming inevitable, the focus shifted from Mosley and the

BUF to other ostensibly more respectable citizens who were known to think well of Nazi Germany. They seemed a more sinister threat. However, as a precautionary measure, Mosley and his wife were arrested in May 1940 and detained under Regulation 18B. They were released in November 1943 because Mosley had developed a blood clot in the leg. After the war they settled in Paris. Mosley wrote his memoirs and emerged unexpectedly to fight the North Kensington seat in the 1959 election where he lost his deposit.

There was an interval. Then in the 1970s Mosley sent a message from Paris inviting me to lunch with him in west London, where he kept a small *pied-à-terre*. On the first occasion we lunched alone, on the second Diana joined us. Perhaps Mosley supposed that the then editor of the *Daily Telegraph* would be able to read the political clock for him. For a man in his late seventies he looked remarkably fit, ate and drank sparingly and left me in no doubt that the spark of hope within him that a call to service might yet come had not been extinguished. Why he thought I could enlighten him I cannot imagine for he had plainly followed the political scene just as closely as I had done.

I left the second lunch with him in Kensington, I remember, and climbed to the top deck of a London bus travelling slowly east. I wanted time to think about our encounter and to ponder the man. The gods had granted him great gifts. He was a magnificent speaker, one of the best of his time. He was good-looking to the end of his days and had many of the qualities people look for in a leader. But then, as is sometimes their way, the gods had decided to mock their handiwork by endowing Mosley with outstandingly bad judgement. That passion of his for fencing tells us something about him. At heart he was a swordsman, not a gownsman – a distinction Harold Macmillan enjoyed making among his political friends and acquaintances. Seen in his early days in politics as 'a coming man', Mosley was defeated by his incurable arrogance. Sensible advice was lost on him. He knew best. Impatience destroyed him. A pity. For, though few will believe it now, he *might* have been a great Prime Minister.

Malcolm Muggeridge

ALL THE YEARS I knew him, that is between 1945 and his death in 1990, I remained fond of Malcolm Muggeridge – yet found him the most exasperating of my friends. As a journalist, he seemed to possess all the gifts to which I aspired. His account of the famine in the Soviet Union in 1933 showed him to be a bold and brilliant reporter. I envied the easy style in which he knocked off leading articles for the *Daily Telegraph* and the astringency of his longer signed pieces. When I returned to the *Telegraph* from the war in November 1945 and was assigned to the Peterborough column, Malcolm was writing leaders in an adjoining room and occasionally dropped off sharp little paragraphs for us. I studied his prose style and sought vainly to match it.

He soon went off to America as our Washington correspondent, a promotion which helped to meet the cost of educating his three sons, but returned to us as deputy editor and resumed, subject to the restraints imposed by Lord Camrose's *Telegraph*, his acerbic long pieces. He occasionally fretted to me about the restraints and our stuffy ways, but in truth Malcolm's writing ran best on a tight rein. He suddenly left us to be editor of *Punch* and, unfettered, put in a controversial spell there – though it lasted five years – ran into trouble by lampooning Churchill and gradually turned towards other outlets.

My exasperation with him, I remember, reached its height after the *Saturday Evening Post* affair. Today what he wrote about the royal family would probably pass unnoticed. In 1957 it was inflammatory and, when ignited by the Beaverbrook press, had Malcolm burning at the stake. Flames of abuse consumed him, which he took badly. One morning when I was travelling to London I encountered a neighbour and mutual friend A. S. Frere, then chairman of Heinemann. He expressed serious anxieties about the effect of this on Malcolm. The attacks, said Frere, were unbalancing him. He might well decide to cast his talents aside and enter the wilderness. He urged me to seek Malcolm out and comfort him.

I did not feel like doing anything of the kind. If only he had remained in our stuffy old office at the *Telegraph*, I reflected crossly and unreasonably, none of this trouble would have arisen. Under the restraining hand of Viscount Camrose, who in those days was editor-in-chief as well as owner, Malcolm's reflections on the royal family would have been tamed and kept him out of trouble.

We had remained in touch, partly because his sons were being educated at Cranbrook, one of many good schools that then lay in my constituency. I had become a Conservative Member of Parliament in 1950, a condition which Malcolm affected to view sympathetically, rather as if I had succumbed to some painful ailment. Yet at one point he was very taken with the idea of offering himself as a Conservative candidate in constituencies occupied by people like Tom Driberg, whom he viewed as fellow-travellers. Win or lose, he reasoned, he would enjoy attacking communist sympathizers.

I had mourned his leaving the *Daily Telegraph* because he had been such a good deputy editor. While continuing to write leaders and scintillating leader page articles, he had taken his duties towards the editorial staff seriously. The job, he once explained to me, was partly fulfilled by loitering on the staircase between the floors of our offices at 135 Fleet Street and engaging journalists who passed by in conversation. By this means you discovered their hopes and ambitions. So many of them, he thought, were as restless as he was. The motoring correspondent longed to report from Paris. The man in charge of crossword puzzles wanted to be a war correspondent. Malcolm set out to uncover some of these dreams. Most of them remained unfulfilled, but by exploring them Malcolm created a bond with some of the staff. This was valuable because the editor Colin Coote, though possessed of a strong intellect, was felt by most to be too Olympian and remote.

With the passing years, my feelings about Malcolm Muggeridge have changed. We tend to be critical of what we do not altogether understand. The course of Malcolm's life is not easily understood, but perhaps his feelings ran through deeper channels than those of conventional people like myself. I think he comprehended the human tragedy better than most of us. His apparent disdain for this earth's prizes was irritating to those of us who aspired to win one or two of them; but it does not follow that his sense of values was wrong. For part of his life Malcolm had been a teacher, and perhaps that is what he did best. He was an influence in my life and I have always been glad of that influence.

In some ways, the early part of Malcolm's life is the hardest to understand. After Cambridge and India and marriage to Kitty, whose aunt was Beatrice Webb, he espoused communism – just when some intelligent people were developing doubts about it – and he determined to go to Russia, perhaps even to settle there. This was not a student thinking of his gap year but a mature journalist of thirty, but neither he nor Kitty had a happy time there. They had difficulty in finding a home, they had very little money and Kitty fell ill. As it turned out, Malcolm saw the light before his employers at the *Guardian*, who used but were not enraptured by his pieces on the famine and made poor use of his dispatches about the notorious Metro-Vickers trial. A number of people, including *Guardian* readers, were not yet ready to admit what Malcolm had discovered for himself about Stalin's Russia. There was a strong tide of thought among otherwise intelligent people that to lose faith in the great Russian experiment was to 'betray the cause' and to fall for the propaganda of right-wing Tories. As a reporter on the old *Morning Post*, which continued to harbour the darkest thoughts about the Soviet Union, I saw both sides of that ideological battle.

I think Malcolm might eventually have prevailed on the Russian front, but he fell out with the *Guardian*, and so returned to India. Looking back on that time, it baffles me that someone of my modest accomplishments could make a living out of journalism, yet Malcolm, infinitely more gifted, had for a time difficulty in making ends meet. Perhaps he was more fastidious about his employers than I was or held stronger views which he refused to suppress. However, he settled down to a solid job in 1935 on the *Evening Standard* Londoner's Diary. It was a hot column in those days, holding a place close to the heart of Lord Beaverbrook who often contributed political gossip to it. Malcolm found working for it boring and dispiriting. Whether working for the *Guardian*, the *Evening Standard* or the *Daily Telegraph*, he found the petty disciplines of a newspaper office irksome. He sought a more literary life and felt drawn to the country where he could settle and write books. This worked for a while and he was unquestionably happier in the company of figures like Anthony Powell and Hugh Kingsmill than among journalists. Most people will sympathize with that. I have never much enjoyed the introspective stuff he wrote at this time, some of which reads too much like a search for the meaning of his own life, but with *The Thirties*, which appeared early in the war, he hit his stride and displayed the best of his satirical writing.

But nothing seemed to afford Malcolm contentment for very long. The Second World War opened up fresh horizons for him, another chance as his biographer Richard Ingrams put it to 'cut loose'. After one or two false starts he joined the Field Security Police, was commissioned in May 1940, did some light cloak-and-dagger work and then, through the influence of Graham Greene, was transferred to the Secret Intelligence Service. At a low point in the war for us, May 1942, he was posted to Mozambique. When I came to know Malcolm after the war, he made light of his time there, treating it as rather a joke. In reality it was serious work because his German and

Italian counterparts were also busy in the Portuguese colony and ships were being sunk off the coast.

He engaged in an unsuccessful love affair, got maudlin drunk one night in July 1943, suffered the torment of a thoroughly bad conscience and decided to end his life. Long after the war, I happened to be in that part of the world and lunched at the café from which Malcolm was alleged to have made his abortive attempt to kill himself. It was, as the proprietor pointed out to me, an exceptionally flat coast with a wide band of shallow water, so when Malcolm set off to drown himself, he had to walk much further than he had anticipated. Exhausted by the effort, he decided to call the whole thing off. He left Mozambique, shrugged off rumours that he had been sent back in disgrace, spent a profitable, if sometimes drunken six months in Paris, blotted his copybook by befriending P. G. Wodehouse and his wife, discharged himself from MI6 and resumed journalism at the *Daily Telegraph*.

My old boss of the Peterborough column, H. E. Wortham – wise, witty, irascible and in outlook thoroughly Edwardian, – used to declare solemnly that you could enjoy wine or women, but to seek to enjoy both led to downfall. One of the mysteries about Malcolm Muggeridge was his success at defying this adage. As all his friends knew, he was a womanizer; and as those of us who drank with him knew, he tippled. Was it boredom? Though as colleagues on the *Daily Telegraph*, we engaged in long discussions on the world about us, I was always nervous of boring Malcolm. He had such a well-stocked mind, though it did not always reach the conclusions that you expected a well-stocked mind to reach.

He was never a *Daily Telegraph* man but he held Viscount Camrose in unfeigned respect. As Malcolm saw, Camrose *was* remarkable; he had turned the *Telegraph* into a prosperous *news*paper and he treated Malcolm very decently, which is why I felt disappointed when *Punch* caught his fancy in 1953. For a while I lost touch with him. After I was given a post in government, he sent me a friendly note, the gist of it being: 'If you really want it, the best of luck.' Very Malcolm.

I have never been sure when Malcolm trod his road to Damascus and changed his life. He had been involved in a protracted affair with Lady Pamela Berry, daughter of F. E. Smith who became the first Lord Birkenhead and wife of Lord Hartwell, Camrose's second son, who had succeeded his father as the *Telegraph*'s proprietor. They took very little trouble to conceal the attachment which became something of a scandal and must have been profoundly distressing even to the long-suffering Kitty Muggeridge. But at some point in 1963 or 1964, I encountered Malcolm in a restaurant. I was with a parliamentary colleague, eating a medium-rare steak and drinking claret. Malcolm eyed me compassionately, lightly conveying the impression that what I was eating and drinking and the company I was keeping were thoroughly bad for my health. He was certainly off the drink then and had perhaps begun his conversion to the vegetarian's diet.

In one sense, it was the right time for Malcolm to mend his ways because he had deservedly become a popular figure with television producers. Those were relatively early days for the medium and the BBC and its rivals were on the lookout for stars. I had seen one or two of his earliest performances, and in 1956 had the luck to catch part of his renowned interview with Brendan Behan. In company with Malcolm, who at that point was still a heavy drinker, Behan had drunk himself into a state of somnolence. Malcolm had managed adroitly to answer his own questions and had kept the show on the road. BBC hospitality, I recall, was more generous then than is permitted today; there was whisky and gin on request. I treasure the thought that perhaps Behan and Muggeridge paved the way for today's BBC sobriety.

A further sign of Malcolm's change of direction came in 1969, when he spent some time in Calcutta with a film crew filming the work of Mother Teresa. I missed the film but read the book he wrote about it, *Something Beautiful for God*, which was published in 1971. He gave the considerable royalties it earned to Mother Teresa. The experience, as Richard Ingrams points out in his biography, radically altered Malcolm's view of Christianity.

> His dialogue hitherto had been conducted with ecclesiastics like Cardinal Heenan. Mother Teresa was completely different. She appealed to him because she was simple and unsophisticated and reduced the Christian Gospel to its bare essentials of love in action. Under her influence, his writing in *Something Beautiful for God* lost the acerbity and slight sanctimoniousness which marred so much of his religious writing.

We celebrated Malcolm's eightieth birthday in 1993 with a small dinner party at the Garrick. He was in better heart than I had known him for a long time. The new life suited him. But memory was starting to play tricks with him. At the suggestion of Richard Ingrams, my wife and I made one or two expeditions with Richard to a little bungalow which Malcolm and Kitty occupied on the Sussex coast. There were always glasses of sherry and beer and a plate of chicken and ham for those who had not adapted themselves to Malcolm's healthy regime.

We would mull over times past at the *Telegraph*. Malcolm's sketches of our more eccentric colleagues were droll – and kinder than I expected. Sometimes his memory faltered, but we got some laughs out of our exchanges.

Our last encounter was during the general election of 1987 in the fine church of New Romney, close to where I live. BBC Radio was doing a series on the ancient churches of Romney Marsh, in which both Malcolm and I shared an interest. We were recorded walking slowly round the church together while Malcolm thought aloud about what we were looking at. 'This programme will have to be heavily edited,' I said to myself after hearing some of his pleasantries.

Malcolm died towards the end of 1990, and in February 1991 was accorded a full requiem mass in Westminster Cathedral. In the absence of Alan Taylor, Richard Ingrams set me to work on the address. I found a vintage piece of Malcolm's early writing in the third volume of his autobiography which related to his days on the *Evening Standard* Londoners Diary:

> Literary paragraphs were turned in by Howard Spring, the book critic, a former *Guardian* star-reporter, with an adoring wife whose praises of him, Neville Cardus once remarked, would have been excessive even if he had been Shakespeare.
>
> In the course of reporting an Empire Free Trade meeting in Manchester for the *Guardian*, Spring referred to Beaverbrook as a pedlar of nightmares. Crozier (*Guardian* editor) ever timid, thought this rather strong and altered nightmares to dreams, thereby procuring Spring an immediate offer of a job on the *Evening Standard* at a greatly increased salary, which he accepted. Later, as a successful

popular novelist, he became a pedlar of dreams on his own account.

Chateau Mugg, premier cru, I called that.

There were plenty of people, including some of Malcolm's friends, who thought it bizarre for such a hardened old sinner to claim conversion to Catholicism. I thought it right to end with a few words in their direction:

> Reflecting on it, I have come to the conclusion that herein lies Malcolm's most valuable bequest to us. For we are offered a welcome reminder that Christ came to call, not the righteous, but sinners to repentance. The life of our friend Malcolm was surely not all that far removed from something at the centre of our beliefs.

Let the cynics say what they will about St Mugg. I believe that is true.

Ian Smith

MY FRIEND PROFESSOR RICHARD Wood of Durban University made a good point in the introduction he wrote to Ian Smith's memoirs, *The Great Betrayal.* In recent years, Wood pointed out, we have been prone to arrive quickly at firm – often unshakeable – opinions of the leading figures of our time. We read so much about them, hear them on the radio, watch them on television and persuade ourselves we know them and can judge them, favourably or otherwise.

Ian Smith? Ah, he was that obstinate old so-and-so who rebelled against the Crown in 1965 by unilaterally declaring Rhodesian independence, and defied Harold Wilson and his successors at No. 10 until 1979, when Mrs Thatcher and Lord Carrington at the Foreign Office finally netted him and secured black majority rule, which resulted in an election which gave Robert Mugabe power. Most people do not know or remember even as much as that, but that is roughly the impression most people old enough to remember when Zimbabwe was Rhodesia have of him. Ian Smith, now in his mid-eighties and surviving precariously somewhere in Zimbabwe, is thought of as an oddball, a relict of the past when the white man sought to rule Africa and as such best put behind us.

I feel more sympathetic than most people towards Ian Smith, whom I have encountered at various points over the years, partly because I admire physical and moral courage – which he possesses in abundance – partly because I have come to see how much his failure came about not only through the misjudgements he made but also because of seismic changes going on in the world outside Rhodesia. 'I perished in the gale of the world,' the Yugoslav patriot Mihailovich is reported to have said before he was executed in 1946. There is a faint echo of that in the political downfall of Ian Douglas Smith.

Taking those points in turn, Smith's physical courage cannot be questioned. During the Lancaster House talks about Rhodesia in London in 1979, Smith called me from his hotel, seeking a change of menu. I took him to a favourite Italian restaurant of mine, where he surprised the waiters by ordering his meal in Italian. He had learned Italian, he reminded me, as a prisoner of war in Italy after his Spitfire had been shot down in the Po valley. He was lucky to be flying at all. While piloting a Hawker Hurricane with 237 (Rhodesia) Squadron in Egypt earlier in the war, Smith had taken off in a misty dawn, hit a bomb shelter and suffered a bashed face, broken jaw, broken leg and shoulder and a buckled back. He was five months in hospital. Over here, he would have been numbered among the Few. So with recollections of some of those Battle of Britain pilots, I find nothing very mysterious in Smith's temperament. Those who reckoned in the mid-1960s that he would be a push-over and would fall in with the designs of the then British government mistook their man.

But the character of Ian Smith, by inclination and profession a successful farmer, is so bound up with the post-war history of Rhodesia that some of this history has to be recited if the reader is to gain any understanding of him. I knew something of the background to the Rhodesian crisis for in 1960 I had taken a long journey with a parliamentary colleague through the Central African Federation. This was a post-war idea whereby the resources of Southern Rhodesia, Northern Rhodesia and Nyasaland would be pooled for the benefit of all three. The great Kariba dam, harnessing the waters of the Zambezi, which I visited several times, would supply power, while Northern Rhodesia contributed the copper belt and its southern neighbour a relatively sophisticated economy. It made sense, but in the late 1940s Southern Rhodesia, having governed itself successfully for twenty-five years, was also making its own bid for dominion status. This was not altogether unreasonable. Its quasi-dominion status had been recognized in 1924 when its affairs were placed under the new Dominions Office, not the Colonial Office, and since 1931 it had been invited to participate in all the meetings of the Dominion, later Commonwealth, Prime Ministers.

But in the 1950s, black African leaders were calling for self-determination. As I had sensed vaguely back in the 1930s while reporting differences within the Conservative party over India, once that cornerstone of empire took the road to independence, many others would clamour to follow. Reluctant to give the Prime Minister of Southern Rhodesia Sir Godfrey Huggins (later Lord Malvern) control of Africans in the area, post-war British governments had settled uneasily on a flawed compromise. It promoted the federation of the three territories, but continued to govern two of them, Northern Rhodesia and Nyasaland, by direct rule from London.

After Macmillan's wind of change speech in South Africa at the end of the 1950s, and with Iain Macleod at the Colonial Office, the pace quickened. Once we agreed to grant Kenneth Kaunda's Northern Rhodesia and Hastings Banda's Nyasaland self-government the federation was doomed. Southern Rhodesia was on its own. Winston Field, who had been leader of the opposition in the Central African Federal Parliament, became leader of the Rhodesian Front party and, after an election, Prime Minister of Rhodesia. He made Ian Smith his deputy and Minister of Finance. I was a member of the Macmillan Cabinet when it decided in 1963 that R. A. Butler should go forthwith to Victoria Falls and wind up the federation. He made a good job of it, but Rhodesia pursued its quest for independence. The British government, perceiving the dangers of ceding full independence to Rhodesia at that point without majority rule, demurred. The African bloc, Butler explained, was becoming more aggressive and threatened to make self-government for white-ruled Rhodesia an issue that would rend the Commonwealth. This was the issue which was to drive Ian Smith and successive British governments apart.

I think it fair to add that Smith and the Rhodesian Front were not opposed outright to giving blacks the vote but, perceiving their state of unreadiness for self-government, thought it should be brought about less hastily. Since the defeat of the Smuts government in South Africa in 1948 and the coming to power of the National party, South Africa had embarked on its ill-starred policy of segregating blacks and whites. Rhodesia had no sympathy with apartheid but accepted that through gradual enfranchisement blacks must be granted a bigger share of government. The trouble in Rhodesia was that this approach fell far short of the aims of black militants such as Joshua Nkomo and others, who were receiving support and encouragement from the Eastern Bloc. Self-government now, they said, or else!

Denied legal independence, Rhodesia moved steadily towards defiance. Ian Smith took over as Prime Minister from Winston Field in 1964, the year in which in Britain the Conservatives lost their first election since 1951 and Harold Wilson's Labour party took over. Early in 1965 Arthur Bottomley, who had succeeded Duncan Sandys as Commonwealth Secretary, made his government's position clear: there would be no independence for Rhodesia without majority rule. Ian Smith came for talks in London which got nowhere, and in November 1965 he made his unilateral declaration of independence. Wilson, talking about an end to the rebellion in weeks rather than months, announced sanctions against Rhodesia. But, given the continued availability of the ports of Beira and Lourenço Marques (now Maputo) in Portuguese Mozambique, and the proximity of South Africa, sanctions did not trouble Rhodesia unduly.

What amounted to a lame siege began. That was when I began to make periodic visits for the *Daily Telegraph* to Rhodesia and became more closely acquainted with Ian Smith. To make the best use of my time, I took an overnight flight to Johannesburg on Saturday, flew up to Salisbury on Sunday, usually in time to attend a magnificent evensong in the cathedral, spent Monday, Tuesday and Wednesday doing interviews or looking round the country, and flew back to London by a late flight on Wednesday. Chris Munnion, our indefatigable correspondent in Johannesburg and Salisbury, invariably included in the programme a visit to the Prime Minister's office.

What became clear to me as time went by was that Ian Smith could not have defied the British government and sanctions (such as they were) for fourteen years without the help and cooperation of most of Rhodesia's blacks. They were not compelled to work for him; his control of the population was tenuous, for most of the Rhodesian army (black and white) was engaged in combating the small but increasing number of terrorists – 'terrs' as the soldiers called them. He depended heavily on black labour for the remarkably successful drive towards self-sufficiency on which Rhodesia embarked. I visited some of the new factories. The white population at that time amounted to around 300,000. They could not have achieved much on their own.

As it became clear that Smith was strong enough to defy the measures taken against Rhodesia, countless illustrious figures descended on Salisbury to reason with him. They included several of Harold Wilson's ministers, Henry Kissinger, Max Aitken (Lord Beaverbrook's son and heir and Smith's former flying companion in Egypt), Lord Goodman and heavyweights from South Africa. There were two meetings with Harold Wilson, the first on the cruiser HMS *Tiger* off Gibraltar in 1966, the second on HMS *Fearless* in 1968. They got nowhere, largely because of the mistrust both men felt for each other. Sir Alec Douglas-Home came out to try his luck on behalf of the Tories. A small commission under Lord Pearce, a distinguished

British judge, came out early in 1972 and concluded in effect that the gulf between what the Europeans and the blacks in Rhodesia wanted was unbridgeable.

Whenever I met the Prime Minister in his office, he spoke hopefully of the talks he was having with black leaders willing to enter a power-sharing agreement. His intentions, I came to accept, were genuine, but those willing to talk, such as the Reverend Ndabaningi Sithole and Bishop Muzorewa, were not strong enough to prevail in an increasingly rough field. The strong men, Robert Mugabe and Joshua Nkomo, were out in the bush advancing their cause by the pugnacious methods that have kept Mugabe in power for twenty years. Furthermore we had not then learned what we know now, that power-sharing in Africa is an illusion. In Africa, winner takes all.

I came to know and to like Bishop Muzorewa, but with hindsight he was never in with a chance against Mugabe and Nkomo. At one point the bishop came to London, called me up and asked if I would care to give him and his small entourage lunch. I took them all to a restaurant in the Strand where the quietest room is below street level and reached by a flight of stairs. The bishop's security guard, who was armed, insisted on sitting at the end of the table facing the staircase. When we ordered our meal, he pleaded duty and declined to eat anything; but when the wine came round he nodded his head. The lunch confirmed my impression that Muzorewa was a good man but insecure.

On one of my visits Chris Munnion arranged for me to spend a day with the Rhodesian army and a day with the elite Selous Scouts. They specialized in making free drops at night from heights at which their planes could not be heard on the ground, thus taking the terrs by surprise. During the ten years of war, mild to begin with then growing in intensity, there were only two awards of Rhodesia's GCV, its equivalent of the Victoria Cross. 'It was our firm policy,' said Smith, 'to preserve the highest standards for our awards; indeed, many people claimed they were too high.' The blacks, I noticed during my time with the Selous Scouts, thought plunging from a great height on a dark night tremendously good value. Smith's Rhodesian army, black and white, contained some wonderfully brave men, but as talks with Smith himself and others brought home to me, they were not going to win an increasingly nasty war.

On another front, Ian Smith was increasingly coming under pressure from South Africa. At the start time of UDI, Rhodesia and South Africa had been allies, with Rhodesia counting on South Africa to take much of the sting out of sanctions. Part of the new pressure from that quarter stemmed from South Africa's ill-fated interest in Angola, where with the agreement of the United States it was planning a major operation against the Soviet-backed MPLA. South Africa itself was coming under increasing international pressure for its apartheid policies and practices. It had battles of its own to fight and, as John Vorster, Prime Minister of South Africa 1966–78 and President 1978–9, warned Ian Smith, his ministers were growing impatient with the Rhodesian problem.

Around the year 1977, after twelve years of isolation, these pressures began to communicate themselves to Rhodesians, who saw in their changing relationship with South Africa the beginning of the end. 'Our position was a lonely one,' Smith was to write later, 'as we strove to persevere with our Western civilization on the southern corner of the African continent.' It is open to anyone to declare that Smith was simply being pig-headed and tightening the noose around his country's neck. I saw it rather differently. He was not a brilliant politician, but his love for Rhodesia ran deep. As I came to see in talks with him, this love convinced him that he knew better than people like Henry Kissinger or our own Foreign Secretary at the time, David Owen, what was best for his country. But isolation prevented him from seeing those changes taking place in the world that were rendering his position untenable. My sympathy for him sprang also from my awareness that his white predecessors had – rather like the old Unionist party in Ulster – ruled Rhodesia for many years without much regard for the future and had made no attempt to bring black Rhodesians into positions of responsibility. There was a divide that surprised me when I first became acquainted with Rhodesia. It was the wealthy, well-connected whites who represented Liberal ideals and bewailed the failure of Rhodesia's white rulers to give the black Rhodesians more opportunities to prove their worth. It was the white artisan class, living a lot more comfortably than they might have done in post-war Britain, who aimed to keep and voted solidly for the status quo. For all these sins of the past and present Ian Smith became answerable. He was the scapegoat. By the time he sought to enlist the help of blacks in government and the government services, the sun was well down in the Rhodesian sky.

A tiny window of opportunity seemed to open in 1978–9 when a deal between Smith and Nkomo looked a possibility. Both our own Foreign Secretary, David Owen, and Cyrus Vance of the United States reckoned they were the only two that could solve the problem. But by then the terrorists were gaining ground. Without much encouragement from any quarter, Ian Smith ploughed on. A new constitution was thrashed out and a referendum on it held early in 1979. There was an overwhelming affirmative vote. In February Smith ostensibly bowed out with a valedictory speech to Parliament. A general election in April brought a 63 per cent turnout of voters, notwithstanding heavy pressure to abstain by the terrorists. On 1 June 1979 Bishop Muzorewa took office as Prime Minister and head of a government of national unity. He would enjoy a couple of months of office before the Lancaster House conference determined that something more radical was needed to end the war.

Mugabe's ZANLA and Nkomo's ZIPRA had brushed the new constitution and the election aside and continued fighting. Jim Callaghan's Labour government lost the election here and Mrs Thatcher took office, with Lord Carrington as her Foreign Secretary. Rhodesia with Bishop Muzorewa in charge was seen as unfinished business. There had been hopes of sanctions being lifted but President Carter of America opposed that. Under pressure from Nigeria and Australia at that year's Commonwealth conference, recognition of the new Rhodesia was also withheld. So to the final act, the conference at Lancaster House in London.

Over lunch in London, Smith and I had a long talk. I knew by then that Mrs Thatcher, Lord Carrington and Sir Ian Gilmour, Lord Privy Seal with special responsibility for Rhodesia, had determined that enough was enough and that if the smouldering conflict was not to erupt into full civil war there had to be an end to it. Smith knew this too. I admired his dignity in defeat. He was bitter at what he viewed as betrayal, but he had a tight hold on himself and I remember leaving our lunch and saying rather pointlessly to myself, 'Yes, this is the only way forward but, dammit, when the call came he did fight for his Queen and country.'

There would be another election under our supervision, with a monitoring force of 1,300 Commonwealth troops, and Lord Soames would go to Salisbury to administer the last rites. I joined the party, and round one of Lord Soames's hospitable dinner tables we discussed the election prospects. There were six principal candidates: Mugabe with his Marxist agenda was expected to win thirty-two to forty seats; Nkomo had the prospect of about twenty; Bishop Muzorewa was thought likely to get between twelve and twenty-two; Ndabaningi Sithole and James Chikerema were not expected to win more than half a dozen seats between them; Ian Smith and the Rhodesian Front were predicted to get around twenty.

Oddly, as I see from notes I took at the time, nobody present predicted that Mugabe would win hands down. We were not as familiar then as we are now with his methods of winning so-called democratic elections. The intimidation was palpable. As the *Sunday Times* correspondent in Salisbury reported at the time, most of the candidates were guilty in varying degrees of intimidatory practices,

> [but] the evidence against Mugabe's Zanu officials and his Zanla guerrilla forces is overwhelming. It comes not merely from the Rhodesian security forces and Muzorewa – that could be expected – but also from his former partner in the Patriotic Front guerrilla alliance, Joshua Nkomo, and more important still from Soames's own election supervisors in the field – the British local government officials and ex-colonial administrators flown in specially.
>
> Their bleak conclusion is that the scale and ferocity of the intimidation carried out by Mugabe's supporters has so

distorted the true pattern of political loyalties that nobody can now know what the result of a free and fair election might have been. This too is deliberate policy on Mugabe's part.

We know now that was nearer the mark than anyone wished to concede at the time. Denied the election, Mugabe would have gone back to the war we were striving to close. He won, as he has won since, through the barrel of a gun. Objections were raised, but the stewards ignored them. Smith had a point when he observed of our Foreign Office strategy: 'Let's wash our hands of Rhodesia, the sooner the better; it has been a thorn in our side far too long.'

Smith took a holiday, returning as leader of the opposition to the new Parliament in June 1980. 'I wanted to do what I could for the country,' he said later, and I think that rings true. We kept in touch, and the last time I met him was at an Oxford Union debate in October 2000. 'I'm younger than you but I look older,' he told me accusingly. 'You've had a lot more to put up with,' I replied truthfully. But it was not the wear and tear of politics that had aged him. In December 1994 his wife Janet had died. She had been his mainstay. 'Her constant interest in and compassion for her fellow men, her moral courage, loyalty and integrity were outstanding,' Ian Smith wrote later. 'These qualities will continue to be an inspiration to me for the rest of my life.'

The *Daily Telegraph* thought it would be good to obtain an interview with him while we were both at Oxford. So when the debate and the receptions were over, we sat down at a table laid for breakfast in Oxford's Randolph Hotel in the early hours of one morning. Mugabe had just threatened to prosecute Smith for genocide. Smith spoke of him, I reported, not offensively but as if he knew for sure that Mugabe had gone off his head. If Mugabe went, he said quietly, there's a future because 'it's such a *wonderful* country'. Ian Smith draws much of his flintiness and resolution from deep love of his country, I wrote. 'He'll never leave it. Like the psalmist, he draws his strength from the hills.' I thought then and I think now, that is the truth.

Helen Suzman

HELEN SUZMAN – WELL-TO-DO, popular and attractive – could have enjoyed a halcyon life in South Africa. Golf was one of her recreations, and the country near her home in Johannesburg abounds with good golf courses. There is also plenty of trout fishing, at which she was proficient. 'I thought up some of my best bons mots as I walked the banks.' Clever, too. After teaching economic history at Witswatersrand University for six years, she would have been welcome in many company boardrooms. Instead of these delights she chose to spend most of her working life in the political wilderness, fighting against entrenched politicians for a cause she passionately believed in: justice for South Africa's disenfranchised non-white population. In doing so she drew against her a wide variety of enemies. South Africa's National party governments and their leaders detested her as a sworn enemy of apartheid and everything that went with it. European South Africans, sheltering and prospering behind the protective arm of Afrikaner intransigence, saw her as a threat to the established order and to their own security. Some abused her as a Jew and a soggy liberal. There were those who took to sending her pornographic literature and pictures of naked black men with naked white women. So that was what she wanted to see in South Africa, eh?

It is hard to think of any politician who chose to take a more uphill road – and to stay on it for thirty-six years. She was returned unopposed for Houghton in Johannesburg in 1953 and delivered her farewell speech to her constituents in 1989. For thirteen of those thirty-six years she was alone in Parliament, the only real voice of opposition to be heard. As I came to know her, I speculated on the attributes that kept her going. One of them was a wonderfully clear sense of perspective. She could not have got under the skin of so many of her political opponents had she not understood them so well.

One evening in the 1970s, Helen and I were guests at a gala party thrown by the late Tertius Myburgh, editor of the *Sunday Times* of Johannesburg. It was a festive evening, with a dinner and ball, winding up with cabaret in which a comedian made everyone laugh loudly by imitating an Afrikaner. Sitting next to Helen Suzman at Myburgh's table, I sensed she was not altogether happy with the comedian's act. Though the scourge of the ruling National party and its policy of apartheid, she did not join the laughter and applause with which this smartly dressed and predominantly European company was greeting mockery of the Afrikaner. Perhaps she felt it was inappropriate. She was opposed to the Afrikaner and all his works, but most of these diamond-studded Europeans were, after all, quietly prospering in South Africa. How much a lively mind adds to a woman's attractions, I thought that evening; though by then she was past sixty years of age, at the balls of long ago her dance card would have quickly filled up.

Her second weapon was her wit. She used a sharp tongue to ridicule her opponents rather than abuse them. Her meetings were well-attended because people enjoyed listening to her sallies. In the election of 1981 I went to one of her meetings in the heartland of her constituency. 'You want to have a meeting?' she snapped lightly at a persistent heckler. 'Why don't you go and hire a hall?' Loud laughter silenced him. Then she turned her sharp blade of ridicule on the Prime Minister, who had recently been trying to say something emollient. 'Now P. W. Botha,' said Suzman, 'cast in the role of a bleeding heart liberal seems to me very extraordinary indeed.' The remark drew much subdued mirth. She was both funny and deadly. The more humour disappeared from Westminster after Winston Churchill retired, the more I came to admire her style.

Not long before she retired from Parliament, one or two of us dined at her home after a day she had spent mainly on the telephone. The unlawful detention of blacks was causing her concern. When any such case was brought to her attention, she would seek out the appropriate authority and enter a complaint. On this particular day she had been in luck. Step by step she had tracked down the chief of police. 'Ah, it's you,' she exclaimed cheerfully when she recognized his voice. 'Oh, it's *you*,' he returned gloomily. She happily recited the story to us. A sense of humour preserved her.

When General Smuts lost the election of 1948, bringing to

an end liberal government, Helen Suzman, looking ahead at what was likely to happen, did think of leaving South Africa. Her husband Dr Moses Suzman, one of South Africa's most distinguished physicians, dissuaded her. Within five years she had cast her lot in with the United party, stood as the Member for Houghton and entered Parliament. Houghton was then a prosperous and largely Jewish suburb in the north of Johannesburg. When Verwoerd became Prime Minister in 1958, her doubts set in again. 'Verwoerd,' she has admitted, 'was the only man who ever scared me stiff. He could talk for two hours in Parliament without a note.' A year later twelve liberal Members of Parliament, including Mrs Suzman, broke away from the United party and formed the Progressive party. It advocated the right of all, regardless of race or creed, to take part in government 'in accordance with their degree of civilization'. She was not seeking universal suffrage but the granting of the right to vote to those with seven years of schooling and two years of employment. That would have immediately enfranchised upwards of 200,000 of the country's 12.5 million black Africans. Then came Sharpeville in 1960, where a protest and the burning of passes led to a riot in which the police first lost control and then their heads. Some sixty-nine blacks were killed and 180 injured, a state of emergency was declared and the African National Congress and Pan African Congress were banned.

When it came to the 1961 election, Helen Suzman was the only Progressive party MP to hold her seat, and was in Parliament in 1966 when Verwoerd was assassinated there. P. W. Botha, then Minister of Defence, stopped opposite her, shook his finger and yelled in Afrikaans, 'It's you who did this. It's all you liberals. You incite people. Now we will get you. We will get the lot of you.' Furious at this accusation, Helen Suzman demanded and through the Speaker received half an apology. She persisted. 'Do you expect me to accept an apology like that?' she demanded of the Speaker. He begged her to calm down. 'What did you expect?' cried Botha. 'There was my leader dying at my feet.' 'I'll tell you what I expect,' said Suzman. 'I expect you to control yourself. You're the man behind the guns in South Africa. You're the Minister of Defence. It would be a sad day for all of us if you can't control yourself.' Botha never forgot that encounter. 'The Honourable Member is a vicious little cat when she is wronged,' he remarked at a later stage. The episode illustrated Helen Suzman's third attribute, her pertinacity.

Between 1961 and 1974 Suzman was the lone representative of the Progressive party in Parliament. Her principal adversaries in those years were Prime Ministers H. F. Verwoerd, John Vorster and P. W. Botha. I never met Verwoerd, but I interviewed both Vorster and Botha for the *Daily Telegraph*. They were tough cookies. 'Down to earth with no pretensions to divine missions' was how she described Vorster. He told her she was worth ten MPs in the United party and warned her against being used too much. There he had a point. As Suzman admitted apologetically to her Houghton constituents, she inevitably became the honorary ombudsman for countless people who had no vote and no MP. They wrote to her in their hundreds seeking help for pass problems, housing problems, bursaries, trading licences . . . Solitary status led to Helen Suzman being overwhelmed by supplicants from every quarter. Vorster's perception of her predicament, however, did nothing to soften her feelings towards him. A Johannesburg *Sunday Times* survey found that 70 per cent of the white population thought Vorster was doing a good job and only 0.3 per cent thought he was no good. Suzman declared she wished to be counted among the minority. In 1974 Vorster asked the world to 'give us six months'. Recently returned from America, Suzman declared he had aroused great expectations there, and as one golfer to another advised him that having made his backswing he had betterfollow through.

Towards the end of Vorster's regime, he sensed that the world – and perhaps also events – were turning against him. He was in defiant mood when I met him. Let the world do its worst, he growled. South Africa felt no obligation to an international community which was treating it as an outcast. He'd had enough of Helen Suzman and there were sharp exchanges. Even the parliamentary correspondent of *Die Burger* felt moved to write a piece: 'Why so hard on Mrs Suzman?' Her relations with P. W. Botha, who followed Vorster as Prime Minister in 1978, were even cooler. 'I place her,' said Botha, 'together with her party, in the position of champion of all those people who contravene the laws and who want to commit crimes against the state . . . she represents all those people who break laws and want to banish order.' His dislike was reciprocated. At one point P. W. was heard to tell Parliament, 'The Honourable Member for Houghton, it is well known, does not like me.' 'Like you?' interjected Helen Suzman. 'I cannot stand you.' Life in Parliament is made easier if one can pass the time of day gracefully with political opponents but Helen Suzman would have none of it. 'God, Helen,' a National party MP exclaimed to her in the lobby one day, 'we can think of ten Progs [Progressives] we would rather have here instead of you – why did they pick on you?' 'For that very reason,' she replied.

One must not leave the impression that Helen Suzman was simply endowed with a sharp line in repartee. Behind her hostility to the National party lay burning indignation at their treatment of South Africa's blacks, and she did more than rail against it. She spent hours in prisons, talking to those she considered oppressed and unjustly treated. On one of her many visits to Nelson Mandela on Robben Island in Table Bay, she was told of a warder who had a swastika tattooed on the back of his hand and imparted the message to his prisoners, 'These are my political views and you will suffer for them.' Suzman wrote to the Minister of Justice, then visited him and warned him she intended to raise the matter in Parliament. 'Dynamite,' he said. Yes, she agreed, headlines all over the world. The minister told her he could not dismiss the man outright but promised he would be gone in a fortnight. Within the time limit, Mandela's lawyer telephoned her; the man had gone.

Helen Suzman saw a lot of Mandela, who inscribed a book for her: 'None can do more than her duty on earth . . .' and she is one of the few people to sympathize with the behaviour of his erratic wife Winnie. As Nelson Mandela himself has admitted, during her long separation from him Winnie took a wrong turning. She became increasingly embittered and unstable, her behaviour culminating in criminal folly. Yet, I noticed, she retained an ominously big following. When I last visited the Nelson Mandela museum in Soweto, she featured more strongly than he did.

There were other reasons, I think, why Helen Suzman's relations with the National party grew more bitter. Primarily, that against all the odds and very slowly she was winning. I saw enough of South Africa in the 1970s to see that influential

Afrikaners were coming round to the view that things could not much longer go on as they were. In quiet conversations running late into the night, we talked this over.

> For while the tired waves, vainly breaking,
> Seem here no painful inch to gain,
> Far back through creeks and inlets making
> Comes silent, flooding in, the main.*

However, the prospect of change did not lead to any relaxation in police control. Perversely a tighter grip was seen to be even more necessary.

The Europeans, who already thought Helen Suzman and her liberal supporters were barmy, felt the rising tension and became more alarmed. There were other pointers. In the Soweto riots of 1976, where 114 people were killed in the first six days and 445 over the months, one factor may have been the threat to impose Afrikaans as a medium of teaching in black schools, but the tinder was so dry that any spark might have touched it off. In November 1977 Suzman told a wildly excited audience in her constituency that like Martin Luther King she had a dream – the Progressive party would become the official opposition at the next parliamentary session. They were returned with seventeen seats.

Helen Suzman consistently opposed sanctions against South Africa – a position which disturbed her relations with many inside and outside South Africa. She believed in contact with the outside world rather than isolation and did not think that measures intended to wreck the economy would improve the situation. She fell out on the issue with Desmond Tutu, who persisted in calling her his 'dear child' though she was

*From 'Say not the struggle naught availeth' by Arthur Hugh Clough.

fourteen years older than him. At the Oxford Union against Donald Woods, she lost a vote on sanctions. At Cambridge against Bishop Trevor Huddleston, she won. She lost marks with some of her supporters by opposing the Drugs Abuse Act of 1971. Knowing there was widespread use of marijuana (*dagga* as it is called in South Africa) among the black population, she reasoned that its prohibition would lead to the jailing of thousands of blacks for what was a cultural habit. It cost her and her party political support. She was once asked by a journalist where the difference lay between her and Margaret Thatcher. Both opposed sanctions against South Africa. Both were tough and did not falter. 'Mrs Thatcher is in power,' replied Suzman. 'I have never been in power . . . Quite a difference.'

But by the 1980s things were starting to turn her way. P. W. Botha had at one point spoken delphically about reform, and in an interview I had with him in Cape Town he made all the right sounds although nothing came of them. Yet it was during his ten-year run of office that the dismantling of apartheid began. The tide of black urbanization and the needs of South Africa's industry were rendering the pass laws inoperable. After Botha suffered a stroke and was replaced by F. W. de Klerk in 1989, the wind of change blew more strongly. Things were changing in the Soviet Union too, which made a difference, for the National party's claim to be the barrier against communism in South Africa now carried less conviction.

None of this made life easier for Helen Suzman. In her last election in 1987 she was embarrassed by a photograph taken of her and Winnie Mandela together. It was published during the campaign, captioned with one of Winnie's most foolish utterances: 'With our matches and our necklaces we will liberate our country.' Suzman exposed the trick but refused to disown Winnie, and was returned with a 5,000 majority. The photograph contributed to her party's loss of seven seats, however, and the role of what had become the Progressive Reform party was once again diminished, although the setback could not alter the direction in which the tide was running.

At the age of seventy-two Helen Suzman left Parliament in 1989, the year F. W. de Klerk took over. In one sense her work was done. In 1990 the ban on the ANC was lifted and Nelson Mandela was released from prison. In 1991 apartheid was effectively abolished. I was in South Africa for the referendum of 1992 in which the white population chose to meet the world's demands and voted roughly two to one for a new constitution reached by negotiation. Then early one morning in April 1994 I got up in the dark and watched the long queues gathering to vote in South Africa's first general election. There came to mind the closing lines of Alan Paton's *Cry the Beloved Country*: 'For it is the dawn that has come, as it has come for a thousand centuries, never failing. But when will that dawn come of our emancipation, from the fear of bondage and the bondage of fear, why, that is a secret.' A secret no longer, I wrote, as the sun rose, the doors of the polling stations opened and whites and blacks moved through them together. For Helen Suzman and her supporters it was the stuff that dreams are made of.

There is no gratitude in politics, perhaps rightly so. Liberal fighters are rarely heroes. Nelson Mandela recognized the debt South Africa owed Suzman in the foreword he wrote to her memoirs, *In No Uncertain Terms*: 'This book relives a magnificent battle against apartheid.' Margaret Thatcher recommended her for an honorary DBE in 1989 and South

Africa awarded her the OM (Gold) in 1997. But Helen Suzman's unerring sense of perspective led her to sum it all up in these words: 'I do not claim any credit for the remarkable changes that have been introduced in South Africa over the last few years. I can only say, to paraphrase Theodore Roosevelt, that I did what I could, where I was, with what I had.'

Denis Thatcher

'THERE IS A LOT of Dad in *Private Eye*,' Carol Thatcher once remarked of her father. The 'Dear Bill' letters composed by Richard Ingrams and John Wells which appeared during Margaret Thatcher's tenure of 10 Downing Street certainly conveyed an impression of Denis Thatcher, though a limited one. Ingrams, editor of the *Eye*, always assured me that I was not the recipient. 'Bill lives in Folkestone and is out of touch with things,' he once told me. But by occasionally dropping clues in the letters which pointed in my direction, he led me to conclude that Bill in Folkestone was one of his little jokes.

Many who read the letters in *Private Eye* took Carol's point. They reckoned they knew just the sort of chap Denis Thatcher was: a genial fellow with one or two slightly disreputable pals, in awe of his wife, fond of golf and even fonder of a glass of gin. That caricature had political value; it made it difficult for journalists to seriously suggest that Denis Thatcher exercised any political influence over his wife's policies. But it was a caricature, not a portrait of the man who, throughout his wife's career, chose a self-effacing role, revealing very little of himself even to friends let alone the news media. In a world in which so many figures on the fringes strive to make themselves a little bigger than they are, Denis Thatcher set about doing the reverse. That made him a hard character to read.

Some of us will remember him not as a man who stood in awe of his wife but as someone who so admired her that, although he had a business career of his own, dedicated much of his own life to her best interests. When we were on golfing holidays and people asked for his autograph, he smiled and signed for them – always with a fountain pen, never a ballpoint – because it was furthering the interests of 'the blessed Margaret', as he sometimes called her. Theirs, one came to see, was a closer partnership than the world imagined.

Denis Thatcher had the knack of reading a balance sheet upside down and then pronouncing on the qualities of a company's directors. It came naturally to him. He was brought up in the family business, a company named Atlas that traded in paint and other products and was founded by his grandfather in New Zealand near the turn of the nineteenth century. Denis joined the business in 1933 and, save for the war years, worked in it for thirty years. After the war, Denis became joint general manager of Atlas on £1,000 a year. In 1947 he was appointed managing director.

One chilly night in February 1949 he met Margaret Roberts, young barrister and prospective Conservative candidate for the socialist stronghold of Dartford, at a dinner party given by Stanley Soward of Atlas. Denis offered her a lift to Liverpool Street station, where she was catching a train to Colchester. The acquaintance fared better than Margaret's chances at Dartford. As Carol writes in the biography of her father, 'Denis says: "She stood for Dartford twice and lost twice and the second time she cried on my shoulder I married her."' Their engagement became known just before polling day in October 1951, when the Conservatives won the general election narrowly but Margaret lost Dartford for the second time.

Apart from Atlas, which prospered, Denis's chief interest was rugby refereeing and administration. As a referee he very nearly attained international status despite an escalating back problem which would later take him off the golf course. Margaret and Denis cannot have seen much of each other in those early days, for he was constantly away on business and she was busy with the law and politics, but in mind and heart they were never far apart. As his wife must have known from their earliest days together, Denis's value as a philosopher and guide lay in deep-rooted common sense. Most of us think we are blessed with common sense until we put our foot in it. Denis Thatcher had more opportunities than any man alive to put his foot in it during his wife's twelve years at No. 10. Furthermore he was under the constant scrutiny of the 'vipers', as he described journalists. Yet he rarely attracted a headline.

Finchley put Margaret's political career on a firm footing by selecting her as its prospective Conservative candidate in 1958. The seat had a Conservative majority of 13,000, which she raised to 16,000 in the general election of 1959. I was sitting just behind her in the Commons when she made her maiden speech in February 1960, but Denis missed it due to business commitments. With 200 on the Atlas payroll, Denis had his work cut out and in 1964 faced a mid-life crisis. 'There's nothing wrong with you physically,' the doctor told him, 'but if you don't stop working so hard, you are going to be very ill indeed.' Denis sensibly took a boat to South Africa, returning to find his wife down in the dumps after the Tories lost the October 1964 election. Atlas was sold to Castrol Oil for £530,000 and Denis got a seat on the board. Burmah Oil then took over Castrol and appointed Denis divisional director of planning and a senior divisional director. 'He took to the oil business like a duck to water,' a contemporary reported.

Being in opposition did not in the long run do any harm to Margaret's political advance. She got a junior shadow post and after the election of March 1966, when Harold Wilson raised Labour's 1964 majority to ninety-seven seats, she became spokesperson on treasury and economic affairs under Iain Macleod. Six years later Ted Heath was not expected to win the 1970 election, but with a late swing he emerged victorious and made Margaret Thatcher his Secretary of State for Education and Science.

No department of government is more set in its ways than Education. As a Conservative minister coming in after six years of Labour rule, Margaret found it hard pounding. I met her once or twice during that period and reckoned she was finding it a punishing experience, more so than No. 10 later on, but political observers found her dogged performance impressive. It also set challenges for Denis. His wife was described in the *Sun* as the most unpopular woman in England. She had ended free milk for children over seven years of age and reversed Labour's policy of forcing secondary schools to become comprehensive. One of the trials for a minister's spouse is having to read and hear harsh criticism of the loved one, and at first Denis found the abuse painful. But he became conditioned to it – and to the loss of her company when she worked long hours. It consolidated a partnership that would withstand the heaviest political storms.

Wilson narrowly won the first election of 1974, which was fought in the artificial light of the miners' strike, on the unsatisfactory question of who governed Britain. Between then and the second election of that year, I was invited to become editor of the *Daily Telegraph*. I had barely taken the chair when Ted Heath's leadership of the Tory party was challenged. It struck me that the *Telegraph* should offer each of those seeking to succeed Heath the chance to state their case, and I commissioned a thousand words from all the runners. Margaret's offering was a professional bit of work, with her thinking tidily assembled by Angus Maude, who had been a journalist. We ran it pretty well as written. It was at this point that I became more closely acquainted with the Thatchers. Margaret acquired from me Richard Ryder, a Conservative parliamentary candidate who was working on the *Telegraph*, as her private secretary, and at my suggestion came along to the *Telegraph* office once or twice to discuss politics with the leader writers. My wife and I lunched with the Thatchers occasionally in their country home at Lamberhurst.

Denis was a sound judge of men, helped by experience in wartime. Having had a glimpse of Hitler's Germany, he had joined the Territorial Army before war broke out. He became an artilleryman, was mentioned in dispatches and made an

MBE. Most of us who took part in the war reckoned it made us better judges of men, and no doubt Denis's business experience helped, as did his work as a referee. He put me right on certain characters more than once, but I cannot remember faulting him. His ability to sum up shrewdly the people he encountered is one of the gifts he brought to the marriage. 'I said to my woman' – as the blessed Margaret sometimes became – 'I said, that chap's a wrong 'un.' He held strong right-wing views on certain topics, but when political life became serious for his wife, his own views were put on a tight rein. He could deliver a good speech because he took trouble preparing it but he avoided talking on the same platform as his wife. A welcome speaker at golfing, rugby and other sporting dinners, he could be counted on never to speak for too long.

It was Len Whitting, a businessman and boss of one of the companies of which Denis was a director, who, just before Margaret Thatcher entered 10 Downing Street, hit on the idea of giving Denis a week's golfing holiday once or twice a year. Whitting and Denis often went to watch rugby at Twickenham together. Ron Monk and I made up the four. Our first jaunt was to Val de Lobo in the Algarve, then in its early days as a golfing and villa resort. The golf courses had recently been created and then, as the villas were built, acted as bait to keen golfers who were encouraged to invest in second homes. Carol has described our first outing. We drove straight from the airport to a golf course and before the sun went down played eighteen holes of the twenty-seven before checking in to our hotel.

In those early days we took our golf seriously. The routine was eighteen holes in the morning, and then, after a pint of beer and a light lunch at the club house, another eighteen holes in the afternoon. After that we retired to our hotel for baths, assembled for a gin or two around seven o'clock and ate dinner together. After the Algarve we did a few turns at La Manga and there made friends with the Ballesteros family. Seve, then the visiting professional there, took a liking to Denis and proposed a golf game in which he promised to handicap himself by driving off one leg. At the last moment, fearing press cameras might catch this exhibition, Denis modestly declared himself an unworthy opponent and handed the baton over to me but consented to walk round.

For some reason I forget, La Manga was temporarily closed on one of our early visits there, but we were treated hospitably and at the end of the week felt we owed something in return. So we invited our friends at the golf club, including Seve, to a dinner at a local restaurant. The party grew and more than twenty of us sat down to an excellent supper. The bill when it came was modest by metropolitan standards, but included a good deal of wine and had to be paid in cash as the plastic card had not yet reached that corner of Spain. The four of us emptied our pockets and found just enough. While we were settling the bill, our guests cheerfully drove off home. We then had to negotiate a taxi back to our hotel on credit, but when we arrived the cash desk had shut down for the night. The taxi driver, reckoning we were bilkers, turned nasty. He would return at 7 a.m. next morning, he warned us, when the hotel cash desk opened. Ron Monk, who had a wonderful way of dealing with difficult chaps, agreed to meet him before the rest of us were awake. 'He went away happy,' he told us reassuringly at breakfast.

Denis had a disarming line in repartee for strangers who hailed him. I recall only one occasion when it failed him. For one of our trips to Spain a friend offered us the use of his private jet. At the last moment Denis was asked whether Paul Daniels the conjuror could accompany us and he cheerfully agreed. Paul would sit in the back of the plane, we were assured, and be no trouble at all. We were given a light lunch and a beer or two by the steward on the plane and dozed off. I awoke suddenly to find Paul Daniels standing over us with a fan of playing cards in his hand. 'Pick a card!' he commanded. 'The look on your face when Paul Daniels woke you up,' I said lightly to Denis later, 'made that a deeply rewarding episode!'

Denis took the episode to heart. 'I believe that chap is coming to our hotel,' he told me gloomily. We speculated on the likelihood of Daniels and his pack of cards haunting our golfing holiday. This became the sort of game boys play at school. 'Cave, Daniels,' I would say to Denis when we caught sight of him. It never failed to startle Denis, but as a bit of fun it also helped him relax.

I look back gratefully on those golfing holidays, which had to be arranged to fit in with Denis Thatcher's inescapable duties as Prime Minister's spouse and company director. They were always fun. We reached our hotel one evening, later than expected because of a delayed flight, to find a dance in progress. They were engaged in a balloon dance, in which couples had a balloon tied round their middles. The object of the dance was to bust other people's balloons by butting them with one's backside. We all took part. Denis's aim always was to do what would redound to the credit of his wife and, on balance, getting involved looked more matey than going to the bar for a gin. So, into the balloon dance.

What I admired in all these encounters was his willingness always to act in the best interests of his wife. He behaved as if he were her ambassador, but never paraded himself as the Prime Minister's husband. People have sometimes asked whether we ever discussed politics. We did, but lightly, and only if he led into the subject. The object of these holidays, after all, was to take some of the weight off his back. I knew how close he was to the political scene. All Prime Ministers need a trustworthy friend with whom when the day has quietened down they can discuss their innermost feelings. Of course Margaret consulted him on issues that troubled her; she could do so freely because she knew he could be trusted. I knew that too, so it was best to keep off such territory. It seemed more relaxing and profitable to discuss why so many of our putts seemed to be drifting to the left of the pin.

When the golf courses in Spain and Portugal became overcrowded we moved to France. There were two courses at Le Touquet we liked. One afternoon there Denis and I gave golf a miss and visited the big war cemetery at Étaples. It is close to one of our base hospitals in the First World War and so contains memorials to soldiers who died from wounds or other causes after the armistice of November 1918. We walked slowly through the long ranks of graves, reflecting on those who lost their lives after the final whistle had blown. A year or two later we gave the south of France a trial, were lent a comfortable villa at Grasse, and played on the championship course at Cannes, with the bonus of a couple of rounds on the course in the hills behind Monte Carlo which, like Cannes, has many British associations. We paid one visit to the United States and played golf on the west coast of Florida, which is quieter than the east.

It would be misleading to present these expeditions as primarily for the benefit of Denis Thatcher and therefore *pro bono publico.* Giving Denis a break from the pressures that fall on the spouses of all Prime Ministers was the pretext for our golf outings, but neither Whitting, Monk nor I were making any great sacrifice on his behalf. We enjoyed playing golf and Denis provided a convenient excuse for taking a week off and playing golf on some of Europe's finest courses.

Some assume that Denis's singular position as Prime Minister's husband was more demanding than for other consorts at No. 10 Downing Street. I am not sure about that. He led a more active life outside politics than most earlier consorts had enjoyed because he had business interests to occupy him. Given his keen eye for a balance sheet and his travels in the world, he earned his fees at the directors' tables, but at one official function overseas he found himself unable to say much to the President's wife because of the language barrier. Margaret, as Prime Minister of course had an interpreter. Denis and the President's wife communicated with each other by drawing little pictures on the tablecloth. There were often situations overseas when the Thatchers were glad of each other's company. At one Commonwealth conference they were housed in new bungalows hastily put together for the event. Margaret came out of the bathroom one morning and remarked to Denis, 'I have news for you. The water is cold.' Denis sat up with a start and part of the ceiling fell on his bed.

His business interests had always to take second place to the social demands of No. 10, but the principal trial for all spouses is the uncounted lonely hours when the Prime Minister is engaged in official meetings. It does not add to the happiness of a man to be told that his wife is engaged in business in which he can play no useful part. I visited him once or twice at No. 10 during such weekends and felt the isolation. But he was blessed, as not all husbands are, with selfless admiration for his wife and her achievements. I suspect he woke up most mornings and gave thanks for the day he married her. No sacrifice, not even of the ego in all of us, was too demanding. He was at one time the proud possessor of a Rolls-Royce of a certain age, which he loved driving. There was nothing flashy about it; he simply enjoyed being behind the wheel of a beautiful piece of engineering But being the way we are, the Conservative leader's husband behind the wheel of a Rolls-Royce troubled the party's image makers, so the Rolls had to be abandoned. By chance we arranged a golf game not long after Margaret's departure from No. 10. We travelled in another Rolls-Royce of a certain age, which he had recently acquired. 'Nice bus you have here,' I said. He purred.

Those who attended one of the lunches, dinners or receptions the Thatchers gave at No. 10 saw Denis at his best. On such occasions the Prime Minister is often busy with the principal guest while other guests may be strangers to each other. Denis would wheel through the room, gathering those who looked solitary under his wing. 'You must meet the Archbishop,' he would say. 'Chancellor, have you met Mr Briggs?' He was an excellent host. All hotel meals with Denis were entertaining not least because he was so particular about the way his food was cooked. 'Waiter,' he would say affably, handing him a plate of steak only faintly pink, 'will you very kindly take this back to the kitchen and tell them to cook it because it's practically raw.'

Which explains why, when she was Secretary for Education, Margaret was seen one evening by the permanent secretary leaving the office early. She was going out, she explained, to buy bacon for Denis's breakfast. There were, the permanent secretary assured her, plenty of people in the department who would be happy to do that for her. No, the bacon had to be just as he liked it, and only she knew what he liked.

That helps us to understand why this was a successful marriage, proof against the fierce light that shines perpetually on 10 Downing Street, proof against the disappointments of life at the top. Assured of breakfasts at which Denis could eat his bacon without complaint, this was a partnership to remind the world what matchless gifts a happy marriage can bring.

Mary Whitehouse

MARY WHITEHOUSE WAS ONE of those souls who feel driven by unseen forces to strenuously contest powerful social trends of their time. She launched her 'Clean up TV campaign' in 1964 just as Britain was cheerfully casting off many of its Victorian inhibitions. The unexpurgated version of D. H. Lawrence's *Lady Chatterley's Lover* had been lawful since 1960, Roy Jenkins was about to become a progressive Home Secretary and Hugh Carleton Greene was getting into his stride as an outstanding and adventurous Director General of the BBC. In his determination to rid the BBC of the old taboos Greene had become a symbol of what Mrs Whitehouse and her supporters found most objectionable about television. As minister responsible for presenting the government's case to the public, I had found his satirical *That Was the Week That*

Was with David Frost and Millicent Martin occasionally embarrassing but hardly corrupting, and, notwithstanding the language, I shared most people's enjoyment of *Till Death Us Do Part.* Both were anathema to the Clean up TV campaigners, which is where some of us differed from Mrs Whitehouse.

But along with many others I shared her forebodings about the impact on children of some of the language used on television and some of the plays being shown. Early in the 1970s I wrote a signed piece in the *Daily Telegraph* contrasting general concern about the pollution of our environment with lack of concern about moral pollution. I thought Dr Benjamin Spock, once the hero of the avant-garde of American parenthood, had a point when he wrote in his book *Decent and Indecent*, 'The abrupt and aggressive breakdown of inhibitions can be disturbing to a society as a whole, particularly to its children . . . This seems more risky when a society already has soaring rates of delinquency and crime, an insatiable appetite for violence on television and what I consider an unprecedented loss of belief in man's worthiness.' In short, Dr Spock did not like the look of the world into which children nurtured in accordance with his theories would have to venture. Pamela Hansford Johnson in her book *Iniquity* published after the Moors murder trial wrote in similar vein about the downward turn aspects of our culture were taking: 'Yes, and raising ugliness all round us. No beauty, terrible or otherwise, is being born. Soho is a nightmare of ugliness, and so is the façade of many a cinema.'

With such thoughts in mind it seemed to me that Mary Whitehouse's movement deserved encouragement and support, even though she sometimes overplayed her hand. So I accepted an invitation to address the first convention of her National Viewers' and Listeners' Association in Birmingham and warned them: 'A comparison with the Pilgrim Fathers is not far-fetched. You set sail in a frail craft towards unknown territory; there are Red Indians on the warpath and a serious risk of being scalped.' Malcolm Muggeridge, who spoke at the second convention a year later, bore me out, describing Mrs Whitehouse as 'pilloried and ridiculed mercilessly without being given the right of reply; the liberal or progressive mind believes in freedom of expression for everyone except its critics'.

From then on Mrs Whitehouse and I met from time to time for lunch or coffee and I would listen to hair-raising tales of meetings with students who roundly abused her for being so stuffy and, as they saw it, seeking to deny them the freedom to liberate themselves. There had been a proper rough house on a campus in Australia where she had spoken. She would recount these experiences not with a whine but in a matter-of-fact voice that I found droll. I admired her sense of humour, still more her pluck.

Mary Whitehouse had been a schoolteacher. As senior mistress of a large mixed secondary school in 1963 she had had a conversation with half a dozen fourteen-year-old girls 'who had been doing things they shouldn't'. 'But *why*?' she asked them. 'Well, miss, we watched them talking about them girls on TV, and it looked as it was easy; and see how well they done out of it, miss, so we thought we'd try it.' She claimed that this and similar tales had brought home to her the immediacy of television. Singling out for disapproval the Wednesday plays on the BBC in which new authors were given the freedom to express their ideas – the so-called 'kitchen sink' dramas – she decided to make a direct approach to Hugh Carleton Greene. At that point relations between the BBC and Mrs Whitehouse took a turn for the worse. Harman Grisewood, deputy to Greene and brother of the better-known Freddie Grisewood of *Any Questions?*, treated her with courtesy but Greene himself had no time for Mrs Whitehouse or her ideas. He was dismissive of those who did not share his outlook. As she wrote in one of her books, *Whatever Happened to Sex*, 'If anyone were to ask me who, above all, was responsible for the moral collapse which characterized the sixties and seventies, I would unhesitatingly name Sir Hugh Carleton Greene, who was Director General of the BBC from 1960 until 1969.'

I was on friendly terms with Greene, partly because he had been the *Daily Telegraph* correspondent in Berlin at the outbreak of the Second World War, partly because while I was in government we had private and informal talks about the licence fee. I sympathized with his anxieties on that score, recalling Cabinet meetings at which the BBC's licence fee appeared at the bottom of the agenda. When the moment arrived for the Postmaster General to join us and state the case for an increase, Harold Macmillan would glance at his watch and adjourn the Cabinet. Over congenial gatherings convened by Harman Grisewood, Greene and I discussed better ways of financing the BBC, none of which forty years on have come to fruition. Now and again, having listened to Mrs Whitehouse's account of Greene's offhand behaviour towards her, I felt tempted to intervene; but I funked it. Intervening in any quarrel between two people with whom you are friendly is risky and, if both are strong-minded, it is very perilous indeed.

Greene was not her only tormentor. She was also the butt for those who saw her either as a damned nuisance or a threat to the public getting what they wanted and so an enemy of liberty. In 1970 Granada's *World in Action* invited her to Denmark to spend a day or two at a sex fair. This proved something of a physical ordeal. She was filmed walking on the battlements of Hamlet's Castle at Elsinore.

> It was sleeting heavily when we arrived and so we bought an umbrella and a five-shilling cellophane 'mac' to go over my coat before I ventured on the last crazy stunt. The high wind tore it to shreds as I struggled to keep my hat on, my umbrella up and my sopping wet feet from slipping on the icy battlements and landing me on the frozen moat below! Then across to the cannons and shots of me looking out to sea with them as my background. Subtle 'right-wing fascist' implications – not a trick missed, I realized afterwards. When I look back on this I wonder how on earth I allowed myself to be persuaded to do it . . .

This led on to her appearance in a programme called *The State of Denmark* in which the participants were called on to discuss the merits of pornography. In sum, a very typical Mary Whitehouse adventure.

She suffered private disappointments as well as rebuffs from the broadcasting establishment, which increased my sympathy for her. The first disaster unfolded at a lunch we had arranged. On entering the restaurant I found that her husband Ernest had unexpectedly joined us. They both looked so woebegone that I called for refreshments. 'This,' said Mary Whitehouse heavily, ignoring her gin and tonic, 'has been the worst day of our lives.' They had spent the morning in court, where one of their sons had been charged with a minor offence – I think over cannabis. Some years later, when I was editing the

Telegraph, there came a second family mishap. One of her children was involved in a divorce. A Sunday newspaper threatened to make a meal of it. Mrs Whitehouse called me to ask if there was any way of averting this. 'It's only news because I'm the mother.' I have sympathy with people in public life who try to shelter their children from the consequences of their own notoriety and, breaking every rule in the book, I rang the newspaper's top man with whom I was friendly. 'I didn't think it was a particularly good story, and that is the only reason I've killed it,' he rang back to tell me later. Parents engaged in moral campaigns are doubly hurt when their children run off the rails.

And some people engaged in moral campaigns think it well to trim their sails a bit when the wind gets up. One reason I held Mrs Whitehouse in such esteem was that she never trimmed. In the forty years I knew her she never changed. It was pointless to attempt to advise her that she was chasing the wrong quarry; the beliefs that drove her overrode all tactical considerations. Her refusal ever to see a situation in which it might be wiser to duck was sometimes exasperating but also estimable. She would discuss books, plays, films and photographs that she condemned as pornographic in clinical detail. One day she summoned me to meet her in the central lobby of the House of Commons to discuss a sexually explicit centrefold in a well-known international magazine over which she had determined to take action. She unfolded this to demonstrate to me its iniquity, ignoring the astonished gaze of one of the policemen who patrol the lobby.

At the root of her campaign unquestionably lay her anxieties about exposing young children to the cruder aspects of sex at too early an age. She strenuously opposed progressive sex education, thought television the wrong medium for it, and did not think that teenage sex would add to the sum of human happiness. 'Public opinion long ago condemned and outlawed the exploitation of child labour by nineteenth-century industrialists,' she is on record as saying. 'Yet, today, our society ruthlessly exploits the minds and emotions of young people for financial and political capital. Children are fodder, not for industry, but for ideas.'

Those who shared her opinions naturally tended to turn to her whenever they saw a book or photograph or television programme which upset them. Her telephone rang incessantly. Then occasionally mine would ring: 'Bill, did you watch that Ken Russell play on television last night?' It is difficult to assess her importance because, as we can see plainly enough, her mission in life failed. The tide against her was too strong. Some may feel inclined to echo the feelings Mary Kenny once expressed in the *Spectator*: 'Look how we treated her . . . and look at us now!' But there are no prizes for foreshadowing doom in what people most want to do. The sense of liberation from the restraints of self-discipline prevailed and still prevails. I supported Mary Whitehouse partly out of a lifelong conviction that Conservatives ought instinctively to know where to throw their weight on the scales. There are times when it is right to push things along a bit, times when it is better to apply the brakes. She was controversial but she was also courageous, and when persuaded to relax over a glass of wine could be a more amusing and entertaining companion than her enemies might ever suppose. There was a hidden depth to her. There must have been. It preserved her from despondency at the failure of her mission.